Design History

B*ismarck!* Very few warship names have the public recognition of this German battleship of World War Two. Perhaps it is because of the British movie *Sink the Bismarck* made in the early 1960s about her hunt, but it is more likely that it was the short but intensely dramatic service career itself that generated so much interest.

Oddly enough, there have been two diametrically opposed schools of thought concerning the *Bismarck* class battleships. One school attributes the *Bismarck* and *Tirpitz* with Herculean properties. The ships were hardly the most powerful battleship design of World War Two but did exemplify the prime characteristic of all German capital ships of the dreadnought era, survivability. It is entirely appropriate that one of the ships was named *Tirpitz* because it was Admiral Alfred Tirpitz, the father of the modern German Navy, who emphasised the primacy of survivability over armament and speed – any warship design is a series of compromises between those three cha acteristics. It may seem obvious, but it wa the belief of German designers that it was far easier to repair a damaged ship than to replace a sunken one.

The second school of thought is that the *Bismarck* design was inferior to her contemporaries and just a rehash the last German World War One battleship design, the *Bayern*. Although it did share the common features of four twin 15in guns, three-shaft propulsion and a similar armour scheme, the *Bismarck* was far removed from the design of the *Bayern*. German battleship design had traditionally favoured toughness – the product of a greater beam, more internal subdivision and thicker armour – over armament and propulsion, but with the *Bismarck* design speed was given almost the same emphasis as protection.

Some critics claim that the designers of *Bismarck* had to start with the *Bayern* class because they had no battleship design experience, since Germany was not allowed

The launching of *Bismarck* on 14 February 1939. Notice the straight stem with the crest at the top of the cutwater. This was similar to the initial bow design of *Scharnhorst* and *Gneisenau*, but as with that pair, the *Bismarck* was subsequently fitted with the raked 'Atlantik' bow.

DESIGN CHARACTERISTICS

Dimensions	Length, oa 813 feet 8 inches (248m); wl 792 feet 4 inches (240.2m). Beam 118 feet 1 inch (36m). Draught 31 feet 11 inches (9.75m) mean
Displacement	41,673 tons standard; 50,129 tons full load for *Bismarck* 42,343 tons standard; 49,778 tons full load for *Tirpitz*
Armament	Eight 15-inch (380mm) guns 4x2; twelve 5.9-inch (150mm) guns 6x2; sixteen 4.1-inch (105mm) heavy AA guns 8x2; sixteen 37mm medium AA guns 8x2; twelve 20mm light AA guns
Vertical Armour	Main belt 320mm; forward belt 60mm; aft belt 80mm; upper strake 145mm; end bulkheads 220mm-180mm; barbettes 340mm; conning tower 340mm; main turrets 360mm on face, 220mm-180mm on sides, 320mm on rear face, 180mm on crown; secondary turrets 100mm on face
Horizontal Armour	Main deck armoured deck 80mm; lower deck armoured deck 110mm sloped to join main belt below waterline
Machinery	Three variable pressure turbines; twelve small water tube boilers, 136,200shp
Maximum Speed	30.12 knots maximum; 29 knots normal operations

to build capital ships in the 1920s and early 1930s due to the Treaty of Versailles. However, the same could be said of virtually all other powers because of the 'Battleship Holiday' imposed by the Washington Treaty of 1922. It may be argued that between 1922 and 1935 Germany had more experience of innovative ship design than all major powers. The Treaty of Versailles, with its 10,000-ton displacement limit, was intended to force any new German battleship design to be an updated pre-dreadnought, grossly inferior to any other modern battleship. However, German naval designers came up with the radically different *Deutschland* class, which they called a *Panzerchiff* ('armoured ship'), but known to their enemies by the more emotive term 'pocket battleship' [for more detail, see No 1 in the *ShipCraft* series].

As remarkable as the *Deutschland* design was, it could not be completed within the 10,000-ton treaty limit. Rather than compromise the design the government chose to hide the actual displacement of the ships. In 1928 another design was drafted for a 19,000-ton battlecruiser armed with eight 12in guns in four twin turrets. This design had very light armour with a 4in belt, but was designed for 34 knots, so nothing like the World War One emphases. Nothing came of it but it does

By the fall of 1939 the fitting of the superstructure was well in hand. Major portions of the superstructure as well as turrets have already been fitted. This photo also provides an excellent view of the bridge wings, which were folded back next to the bridge when not in use.

Bismarck with bridge wings extended. The support structure for these wings on *Bismarck* was solid while those on *Tirpitz* had an open lattice structure. The ship is still missing items of equipment but the new Atlantik bow with its stem-head anchor is apparent. Notice also the protective fairing under the port anchor hawse.

show that German naval designers were not in hibernation, and were not hidebound. In 1932 a series of design studies was prepared for a 35,000-ton battleship.

Two improved *panzerschiffe* were ordered before Adolf Hitler came to power in 1933, when the navy was redirected towards ships suited to Germany's Baltic needs. At this time his intent was not to challenge the Royal Navy, but he authorised the construction of two more *panzerschiffe* with an increased protective scheme and displacement. When France announced the construction of the *Strasbourg* in 1934, German naval staff changed the requirements for the fourth and fifth ships to be armed with nine 11in guns. Orders were placed for two ships of the much heavier 26,000-ton design in February 1934, but building plans had to wait until the Anglo-German Naval Treaty was signed on 18 June 1935. This allowed Germany to build up to 35 per cent of the strength of the Royal Navy, but also bound Germany to follow the restrictions of the 1922 Washington and 1930 London Treaties. These of course limited battleships to 35,000 tons but allowed 15in guns, and the Germane naval staff wanted to mount six of these in three twin turrets in the new ships. Hitler, however, did not want to antagonise the British and decided to keep to 11in guns.

These two ships emerged as *Scharnhorst* and *Gneisenau* and were always rated as battleships by the German navy. Some have classified them as battlecruisers due to their comparatively light armament and high 30kt speed, but the design had a battleship level of protection, with maximum belt thickness a little less than 14in. Although intended to combat the French *Dunkerque* class battlecruisers, if anything, the *Scharnhorst* class carried forward the design emphases of the Imperial German battleships, sacrificing gun power in favour of increased protection and speed. As first conceived the *Scharnhorst* design was to displace 26,000 tons but as completed they actually displaced a little over 31,000 tons standard. Now it was time for the designers to develop a design fully up to London Treaty limitations.

The 1932 design studies for a 35,000-ton battleship were built around a ship capable of 30kts, with good armour protection and armed with eight 13in (330mm) guns in four twin mounts. At the time this was yet another design to counter the French *Dunkerque* class, but before a new design had been settled both France and Italy announced that they would start construction of 35,000-ton battleships armed with 15in (380mm) guns. Italy laid down the *Vittorio Veneto* in October 1934, followed by the French *Richelieu*, laid down in October 1935. In light of these developments Hitler ordered the new battleship design to mount 15in guns also. However, to achieve a 30kt speed and with the required level of protection would require ships of a far heavier displacement than 35,000 tons. *Bismarck* was laid down on

Tirpitz in June 1941 with turret crowns and 15in guns painted dark grey.

This is a starboard quarter view of *Tirpitz*. The ship is easily distinguished from *Bismarck* by the shelter deck extending to the hull sides amidships and the mounting of the aircraft/boat cranes one level higher on that shelter deck.

1 July1936 by Blohm & Voss at Hamburg, with *Tirpitz* following on 20 October 1936 at the Wilhelmshaven Navy Yard.

Germany had promised to honour past and future naval agreements, so when the new London naval treaty of March 1936 limited main armament in new construction to 14in guns the new *Bismarck*, which would be laid down four months later, would clearly violate those terms as well as the earlier displacement limit. However, the Treaty had an escalator clause, which stipulated that maximum displacement could jump to 45,000 tons and main armament to 16in guns if Japan and Italy had not signed the treaty by 1 April 1937. The German admirals felt confident that neither power would sign, and accordingly gambled that the *Bismarck* would be legal when completed under the escalator clause – and they were right. Great Britain went the other way and gambled that the treaty would be signed, so the five new battleships of the *King George V* class went with the lighter 14in gun on a 35,000-ton design, although as completed they came in at around 37,000 tons standard.

A cursory comparison of the statistics for and *Bismarck* emphasises that the latter was not a reworked World War One design.

The *Bismarck* hull amounted to 25 per cent of displacement, while the hull weight of the *Bayern* exceeded 30 per cent. Belt armour for *Bismarck* was less than *Bayern* but deck armour was almost four times as great (the main armour belt on *Bismarck* was actually thinner than *Scharnhorst*'s), but this new Krupp armour had a 25 per cent greater resistance capability than armour of the First World War. The 14.96in (380mm) guns were of a completely new design and longer barrel length. However, unlike most other modern designs, the *Bismarck* did not adopt the all-or-nothing armour scheme. It was almost there with a deep, long main belt but light belts ran along the waterline from the ends of the main belt to the cutwater on the bow and aft to the stern, and there was also an upper thinner strake of armour above the main belt.

Two armoured decks were provided with the upper armoured deck carrying 1.97in (50mm) of armour along the entire deck. The lower and heavier armoured deck was 3.15in (80mm) in thickness increasing to 3.74in (95mm) over the magazines in *Bismarck* and 3.94in (100mm) over the magazines in *Tirpitz*. The lower armoured deck had the traditional turtleback shape with sides of the deck sloping down to join the main armour belt underneath the waterline. In theory the area below this deck, which protected the propulsion plant, magazines and other vital operational stations, would be very difficult to incapacitate and the protected area would provide for reserve buoyancy for stability of the hull. USN calculations compared the protection afforded by the German armour layout of *Bismarck* against the penetration power of the 16in/45 American AP shell. The results reflected an immunity zone for the German propulsion plant from 11,000m to 21,000m. The protection was even more impressive over magazines, as they were immune from penetration from 25,000m to point blank range. With a beam in excess of 118ft, only 3ft less than the far heavier Japanese *Yamato* class, the *Bismarck* design excelled in subdivision. As constructed, the *Bismarck* had an almost straight stem, similar to the cutwaters of *Scharnhorst* and *Gneisenau* as built, and would have been a very wet ship if operated without the revised 'Atlantik' bow. Welding was used for about 90–95 per cent of the construction of the pair.

Bismarck did share the three-shaft propulsion arrangement of the *Bayern*, but this was merely a design decision, rather than copying the older design, which could not have coped with *Bismarck*'s 30kt maximum speed. The two outboard shafts were of traditional design but the centreline shaft was surrounded by a streamlined skeg before exiting the hull. One design characteristic that was to haunt the *Bismarck* was the rudder arrangement. Twin rudders were chosen, but instead of straight rudder posts, they angled inward at eight degrees, imposing unequal weights and stress on the rudder housings.

Tirpitz with navigation bridge wings extended. Notice the lighter weight open lattice wing supports, compared to the solid support structure on *Bismarck*.

The German designers mulled over various propulsion fits. The economy and range conferred upon the *panzerschiffe* by use of diesel engines sorely tempted the designers, but diesel technology could not provide 30kts. Then the designers looked at turbo-electric drive as installed on the USN battleships of the *California* and *Colorado* classes, and the record-breaking new French liner *Normandie*. This system had many advantages: with electric drive motors separated from the turbine generators, shorter shafts could be used, which reduced vibration, eliminated gearing so control was much more efficient, and turbines could be simplified. The down side was additional weight and highly vulnerable electrical cable supply to the electric motors. Nonetheless, the turbo-electric system was selected for the *Bismarck*, but it could not meet the requirement for an incredibly short transition time from full ahead to full astern of under 20 seconds. The main designers were also developing second thoughts about turbo-electric drive, since it required much more maintenance than traditional steam plants and was far more difficult to repair. The weight saved by using all-steam propulsion could go into additional armour, while the potential unreliability of turbo-electric finally convinced the

ARMAMENT CHARACTERISTICS

Ordnance	Purpose	Horizontal Range	Elevation/Vertical Range	Rate of Fire RPM	Shell Weight
380mm/L47 (14.96-inch)	surface	39,590 yards; 36,520m	30 degrees/NA	3	1,764lbs; 800kg
150mm/L55(5.9-inch)	surface	25,153 yards; 23,000m	40 degrees/NA	6	99.8lbs; 45.3kg
105mm/L65 (4.1-inch)	DP but primarily heavy AA	19,357 yards; 17,700m	85 degrees/12,500m	15	33.3lbs; 15.1kg
37mm/L83 SK C30 (1.46-inch)	Medium AA	7382 yards; 6750m effective	80 degrees/6800m maximum/4800m effective	160 maximum 60 operational	1.64lbs; 0.745kg
20mm (0.79-inch)	Light AA	5,249 yards; 4800m	90 degrees/4800m maximum/3700m effective	280 maximum 120 operational	0.291lb; 0.132kg
533mm (21-inch) **torpedo tubes** – *Tirpitz* only	Sub-surface	6000m at 44 knots 8000m at 40 knots 14,000m at 30 knots	NA	NA – sixteen reloads	1,538kg

ARADO 196 A3 RECONNAISSANCE FLOATPLANE CHARACTERISTICS

Maximum Speed	Ceiling	Range	Powerplant	Armament
193 miles per hour	23,000 feet	670 miles	970hp BMW 132k nine-cylinder radial	Two 20mm cannon in wings; three 7.9mm MG17 machine guns, one forward and two for rear gunner: two 110lb bombs

designers in favour of a very advanced steam turbine power plant.

When it came to armament, an entirely new 380mm/47 Model 1934 heavy gun was designed and built by Krupp. This new gun had a much greater range than the 380mm/45 guns of *Bayern* (36,520m at 30 degrees elevation compared with 23,200m at 20 degrees). Krupp designers had also developed a 16in (406mm), but in the interest of a speedy completion the 380mm gun was ordered for the *Bismarck* class. German designers did consider triple and even quadruple main gun turrets, but the traditional twin gun turret was selected for simplified ammunition stowage and delivery.

Many writers have criticised the selection of single purpose 5.9in (150mm) secondary guns and separate 4.1in (105mm) heavy AA guns as archaic and inefficient, but the modern battleship designs of Italy, France and Japan also featured surface action secondary batteries and separate tertiary heavy AA guns. Only the Royal Navy and the USN gravitated towards dual-purpose secondary guns. Another fallacious criticism of the *Bismarck* design was a weak light AA fit. One only needs compare ship designs at the same point in time to disprove this argument. The *Bismarck* already mounted 105mm heavy AA, 37mm medium AA and 20mm light AA guns with four HA directors (designed for six HA) in early 1941 when USN battleships had only 5in heavy AA/DP, inadequate 1.1in or no medium AA and only machine gun light AA.

As it was, the *Bismarck* class battleships were the heaviest and most capable European battleships ever built.

Another view of *Tirpitz* in early summer 1941. At this early stage in the ship's career, the main identifying features are the lattice support structure of the stowed bridge navigation wing and the shelter deck extending to the hull edge for a short length.

Careers

There were two ships in the *Bismarck* class and their very different careers make their names seem appropriate. Otto von Bismarck was Prussia's Iron Chancellor, whose leadership eventually unified the numerous German states into the German Empire or Second Reich. His success was spectacular and the battleship named after him enjoyed the most spectacular naval success of the Third Reich. However, unlike the chancellor, the ship quickly came to ruin. The driving force behind the High Seas Fleet of the Second Reich was Admiral Alfred von Tirpitz, and the toughness and survivability of the Imperial German battleships is a direct result in his emphasis on a ship's survivability. He was also a strong proponent of the Fleet in Being theory – that as long as an inferior naval power had a fleet, it could tie down far larger naval forces just through the threat of action. The battleship *Tirpitz* exemplified both theories of her namesake. The *Tirpitz* was assaulted by more aircraft than any other warship in World War Two and her toughness enabled her to survive for 3½ years before succumbing. Likewise, the mere existence of *Tirpitz* tied down disproportionate allied naval power. *Bismarck* lived and died by gunfire but the *Tirpitz*, lurking in the Norwegian fjords, caused more damage to the allied war effort by her latent threat than any other German surface ship.

BISMARCK – THE GREAT HUNT

Of the 178 all-big-gun battleships built by the world's navies from the *Dreadnought* onwards, the one with the shortest service life was the *Bismarck*. Commissioned on 24 August 1940 and sunk on 27 May 1941, her career spanned a mere nine months. However, she became legend in that short time.

When commissioned at Hamburg *Bismarck* was still short of some essential equipment (transferred to Russia as part of the Soviet-German Non-Aggression Pact), so she did not sail for Kiel until 14 September 1940. October and November were spent in the eastern Baltic intensively testing machinery and weaponry, return in December for more yard time at Kiel and Hamburg. A severe winter delayed her return to the Baltic until 6 April 1941 to finish her trials, as the cold made it very difficult to remove a sunken merchant ship from the Kiel Canal. On 1 May 1941 Adolf

Bismarck taking on supplies at pier-side in March 1941 before steaming into the Baltic for trials.

Bismarck at Grimstadfjord, Bergen, Norway. She still wears her Baltic paint scheme.

Bismarck seen from *Prinz Eugen* during their joint manoeuvres in the Baltic in April or May 1941.

This is another view of *Bismarck* at Bergen taken from *Prinz Eugen* (in the foreground).

Hitler came aboard for a formal inspection, after which he went over to the *Tirpitz* at Gotenhafen.

The story of the *Bismarck*'s first and only sortie – Operation Rheinübung – has been often told and will be familiar to most readers so only a reminder of the main events is given here. Setting out for Bergen in Norway on 19 May, flying the flag of Admiral Gunther Lütjens, *Bismarck* rendezvoused with the heavy cruiser *Prinz Eugen*. As they were steaming through the confined channel of the Kattegat, separating Denmark from Sweden, *Bismarck* was sighted by the Swedish cruiser *Gotland*, and this information quickly found its way to London. While at Bergen a reconnaissance Spitfire caught the German force in photographs on the 21st, and having not refuelled as planned, the

Bismarck sailed the same evening.

There was an oiler stationed off northern Norway for refuelling *Bismarck* but again Lütjens decided not to top off *Bismarck*'s tanks, believing that his breakout had not been spotted. However, the Royal Navy had already made dispositions to block the passages into the Atlantic, and when Lütjens entered the Denmark Strait (the gap between Greenland and Iceland) on the 23rd, his ships were spotted by the radar-equipped cruiser HMS *Suffolk*, which quickly sent out a contact message to the Admiralty. A second British heavy cruiser, the *Norfolk*, joined later, and in firing at the latter, the blast of *Bismarck*'s salvos damaged her own forward radar, so *Prinz Eugen* was ordered to take the point.

Unable to shake off the shadowing cruisers, the German force was intercepted early on 24 May by the battlecruiser HMS *Hood* and the new battleship *Prince of Wales*. At 5:52am at the range of 26,500m *Hood* was the first to open fire, followed a minute later by *Prince of Wales*. Initial fire was on *Prinz Eugen*, which was misidentified as *Bismarck* because of the intentional family resemblance of Kriegsmarine construction. The British ships steamed directly towards the Germans in order to close the range, since Admiral Holland, the British commander, recognised that *Hood*'s weak deck armour was vulnerable to plunging fire but her belt armour was better able to resist direct horizontal fire. He had closed to 16,500 yards by 6:00am when he ordered a turn to port. At this point in time the Kriegsmarine achieved its greatest surface action victory.

A Royal Navy Board of Enquiry determined that the first two salvos from *Bismarck* bracketed *Hood* and that the third salvo straddled the ship. A 15in shell hit near the port twin 4in gun position just forward of the mainmast. This started a fire on the shelter deck with not only the 4in ready ammunition but also the UP mounts and pom-poms. The fourth salvo fell astern but the fifth was again on target. There was at least one hit somewhere around the mainmast followed by a catastrophic explosion of the aft magazines. The official verdict was that the aft 4in magazine exploded first and that this explosion detonated the aft 15in magazines and blew out a huge area of the lower hull.

Prince of Wales was also damaged and turned away, but rather than go after the wounded battleship Lütjens ordered that the breakout continue. *Bismarck* had not come through unscathed. There had been three 14in shell hits from *Prince of Wales* on *Bismarck*. One was at the bow, above the waterline but beneath the bow wave, which caused forward compartments to flood; even worse, a fuel line was cut and 1000 tons of fuel oil in the forward tanks could not be used. A second hit was amidships below the waterline but did no significant damage. A third hit amidships destroyed the Admiral's launch and severed a compressed air pipe, which precluded use of the aircraft catapult. After evaluation of the damage, Lütjens decided to head *Bismarck* for France because of the fuel situation but for *Prinz Eugen* to continue the raid. *Bismarck* covered the separation of the two ships, exchanging fire with *Prince of Wales* and *Suffolk*, but no hits were scored by either side.

On the evening of the 24th the carrier *Victorious*, part of a separate force under Admiral Tovey in *King George V*, launched nine Swordfish torpedo bombers against *Bismarck*. One torpedo hit the main belt amidships on the starboard side, the shock exacerbating the existing damage and flooding a boiler room. Early on the 25th *Bismarck* turned for her run to France and, although Lütjens did not realise it, contact was broken. The *Bismarck* was not reacquired until 10:30am on May 26, when she was sighted by a Catalina flying boat only 690 miles from Brest and 24 hours from the probable safety of Luftwaffe protection. No British surface ship was in position to inter-

One of the most famous photographs of *Bismarck* is this one taken from *Prinz Eugen* showing her firing her main guns in her first salvo at *Hood*.

Bismarck down by the bow from the result of a 14in shell strike from *Prince of Wales* which flooded some forward compartments. What is not visible is that the same hit precluded the *Bismarck* from using 1000 tons of fuel oil in forward storage compartments. Also, the over-painting of the hull Baltic scheme to a monochrome grey is evident.

BISMARCK CLASS KEY DATES

	Laid Down	Launched	Completed	Fate
Bismarck	1 July 1936	14 February 1939	24 August 1940	Sunk 27 May 1941
Tirpitz	20 October 1936	1 April 1939	25 February 1941	Sunk 12 November 1944

cept, which left only the carrier *Ark Royal*, approaching from the south, to launch a series of Swordfish torpedo attacks on *Bismarck*. The German ship seemed to come through all of them and shrugged off two torpedo hits amidships, but a third torpedo in the evening attack exploded on the port side underneath the steering-gear room just as the *Bismarck* started a turn to port. The explosion jammed the rudders at 12 degrees to port, and although the starboard rudder was disengaged the port rudder remained unmoveable. The lack of steering control sealed the fate of the ship.

By the evening her speed was down to around 9kts, and during the night she was attacked by a British destroyer flotilla, which launched sixteen torpedoes but, despite being barely manoeuvrable, *Bismarck* was not hit. *Norfolk* regained contact on the morning of 27 May and vectored the British battleships *Rodney* and *King George V* towards their target. At 8:47am *Rodney* opened fire and *KGV* at 8:48 at 18,000m. The *Bismarck* replied at 8:49, the first two salvos bracketing *Rodney* and the third straddled her, but then *Bismarck*'s accuracy fell off rapidly, due to an 8in shell hit from *Norfolk* on *Bismarck*'s forward director. During the action it was the *Rodney* that dealt out the bulk of the punishment as her 16in shells caused far more damage than the 14in guns of *KGV*. Although *Rodney* closed to 2400 meters, the main belt of *Bismarck* was never penetrated, but the lighter strake of armour above the main belt was thoroughly perforated and all guns were silent by 9:31am. British fire continued at increasingly closer ranges until 10:22 when *Dorsetshire* was ordered to finish off the *Bismarck* with torpedoes. At 10:00 it was ordered to scuttle the *Bismarck* and scuttling charges were detonated at 10:20am. By 10:40 she had sunk.

TIRPITZ, LONELY QUEEN OF THE NORTH

Unlike *Bismarck*, *Tirpitz* never had any spectacular victory. During her three and a half year service history she was a regular target of RAF, FAA and RN attacks, most of her time being spent hiding in one Norwegian fjord or another with only brief periods at sea. Yet, for all of her lack of action, the *Tirpitz* made a greater contribution to the German war effort by her latent threat than the spectacular sortie of *Bismarck*.

Early in 1941, even before completion, *Tirpitz* had become a prime target of intensive aerial attack by the RAF, which mounted five separate night raids between January and March 1941 involving 359 medium bombers, but the ship was never hit. The *Tirpitz* commissioned on 25 February 1941 and on 9 March sailed to Gotenhafen (Gydnia) in the eastern Baltic, where for almost three months she would undergo her trials. During the voyage she hit 29kts.

In late May it was decided to send her back to Kiel for additional equipment, where she was once again within range of the RAF. In May, June and September raids were conducted against *Tirpitz* but, as in the earlier attacks, no hits were scored. On 23 September 1941 *Tirpitz* again sailed eastward, but this time on a combat assignment. Germany had invaded Russia in June and the mission of *Tirpitz*, as flagship of the Baltenflotte North Group, was to prevent the Soviet Baltic Fleet from breaking out. With the *Admiral Scheer*, *Tirpitz* was to attack Kronstadt, the Soviet base just west of Leningrad, but by then Luftwaffe attacks had neutralised the Soviet fleet, and the battleship returned to Gotenhafen. On 13 November 1941 Hitler

Tirpitz in Baltic trials with guns at maximum elevation. In contrast to *Bismarck* the stack cap of *Tirpitz* is painted black.

This shows the *Tirpitz* with the camouflage scheme that she wore from May to August 1944. The hull, Anton and Dora turrets, the barbettes to Bruno and Caesar turrets, and the shelter deck are painted a very dark grey with lighter grey for the superstructure.

met with Admiral Raeder, who suggested the movement of *Tirpitz* to Norway in order to attack the Murmansk convoys, as well as to protect against a rumoured British invasion of Norway. Hitler agreed, as long as the ship did not attack any convoy escorted by an aircraft carrier.

Operation *Polarnacht* was the transfer of *Tirpitz* to Norway and was well named as indeed *Tirpitz* moved into the realm of polar nights, long in the winter, short in the summer. On 15 January 1942 *Tirpitz* sailed from Germany for the last time to a berth in Faetenfjord near Trondheim. The British knew of the deployment through Ultra intercepts, but because of successful camouflage and short days could not initially find the battleship. Only four-engine heavy bombers had the range, but in the course of the spring, commencing on the night of 29 January 1942, five raids were carried out by a combined total of 155 Halifax, Stirling and Lancaster bombers, all with no damage to *Tirpitz*.

Norwegian operations by *Tirpitz* were to be constrained by low fuel supplies, and a planned attack on convoy PQ8 in late January was cancelled for this reason. In February *Tirpitz* was placed on alert to support the 'Channel Dash' of *Scharnhorst*, *Gneisenau* and *Prinz Eugen*, but was not required. On 24 February 1942 *Tirpitz* raised the flag of Vice Admiral Ciliax as commander of Group North, initially consisting of *Tirpitz*, *Admiral Scheer* and *Prinz Eugen*, although the last was not operational due to a submarine torpedo hit.

In early March 1942 *Tirpitz* and three destroyers sortied to intercept convoys PQ12 and QP8, but thanks to Ultra intercepts the convoys were re-routed and *Tirpitz* just missed contact, but *Tirpitz* was attacked unsuccessfully by torpedo bombers from *Victorious*. It took until June

Tirpitz during main battery trials in the Baltic. It can be determined that this is *Tirpitz* by the Dopp. L. C/31 4.1in gun mount. Although this was later replaced by the purpose built Dopp. L. C/37, the aft pair of these mounts in *Tirpitz* initially had the interim design, whereas *Bismarck* had the larger Dopp. L. C/37 mount in this position from the start.

Above: *Tirpitz* is seen in January 1942. This is evident by the two single 20mm guns on top of the forward bridge, which were landed in February 1942 for a quad 20mm.

for enough fuel stocks to be accumulated for another sortie, when *Tirpitz*, *Scheer*, *Lützow*, *Hipper* and destroyers were sent to intercept convoy PQ17. Although the surface ships were recalled on July 5, the mere threat led to the order to disperse the convoy, which was then decimated by U-boats and the Luftwaffe. That summer *Tirpitz* moved to Narvik, further north and out of RAF range. The ship needed an overhaul but Hitler insisted that she stay in Norway, so Trondheim was slowly equipped for this process. The overhaul was conducted in stages, so *Tirpitz* would be immobilised only for short periods of time, but the work was completed on 28 December, when *Tirpitz* started a series of trials reaching into January 1943.

Scharnhorst joined *Tirpitz* and since there were no Russian convoys in the first half of the year, the pair was ordered to attack allied facilities on the island of Spitzbergen. On 8 September 1943 *Tirpitz* fired her main guns at an enemy for the first time and all land targets were destroyed. The British had planned an underwater attack using human torpedoes in October 1942, but it was aborted before reaching Norway. A more successful operation was mounted the following September, involving ten X-Craft midget submarines towed to Norway by fleet submarines. On September 22 two of them, *X-6* and *X-7*, penetrated the anchorage and laid four two-ton mines underneath the battleship, causing significant damage to the hull and equipment, some distortion, and the influx of 1500 tons of seawater. Turret Dora was lifted off its roller track and jammed, while shock damage to the turbines immobilised the ship. Repairs were necessarily undertaken in situ by the repair ship *Neumark*, and lasted from November until February 1944. *Tirpitz* then underwent a new series of trials in March and April.

As soon as the *Neumark* left, the Royal Navy scheduled a new attack on *Tirpitz* by the Fleet Air Arm (FAA) in Operation Tungsten. On 3 April 1944 a combined strike of 40 Barracudas from *Victorious*, *Furious*, *Emperor*, *Searcher*, *Fencer* and *Pursuer* was launched in two waves, catching the *Tirpitz* unprepared. Escorting Corsairs and Hellcats machine-gunned the

Right: *Tirpitz* at Faettenfjord in the spring of 1942, dated by the dark grey stern. She wore this scheme only from March to April 1942.

Opposite, top: A beautiful study of *Tirpitz*'s forward superstructure in a Norwegian winter, 1942.

Opposite, bottom: The *Tirpitz* proved very difficult to spot, as she was constantly repainted to adjust to the surrounding terrain. This photograph shows her around March/April 1942 before her camouflage acquired irregular splotches.

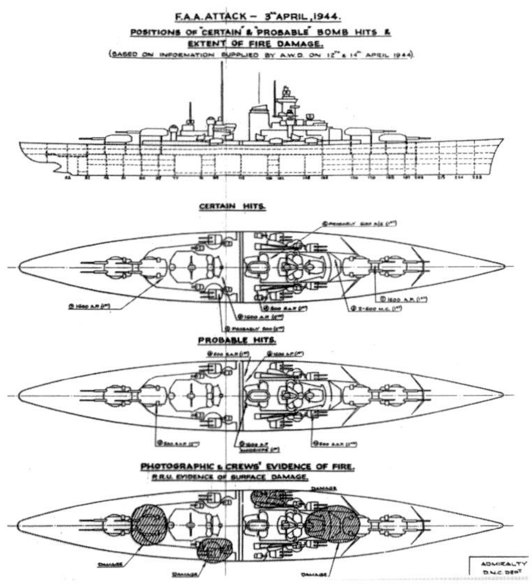

Above: Two Albacores from *Victorious* press home their attack on *Tirpitz*, 9 March 1942.

Above, right: British naval intelligence assessment of damage from the Tungsten raid. It proved quite accurate.

Below: *Tirpitz* at Altafjord showing the camouflage pattern that she wore in the early fall 1943.

ship as the Barracudas dropped 1600lb bombs. The operation was one of the best-executed missions of the FAA during the war, fourteen bomb hits causing serious damage. Further FAA attacks during the late spring were cancelled because of cloud cover, or else were unsuccessful because of the smoke screen over the ship. The culmination of the carrier assault on *Tirpitz* came in Operation Goodwood with attacks on 22, 24 and 29 August. Two further hits were scored but on the whole the operation was foiled by smoke screens over the target. It was decided that the ordnance carried by British naval bombers was just not powerful enough to sink the *Tirpitz*. Something bigger was needed.

A new aerial weapon became available in 1944 – the 12,000lb 'Tallboy' bomb filled with Torpex, which could only be carried by specially modified Lancasters. In the summer of 1944 *Tirpitz* was still anchored at Kaafjord, just outside of the combat range of the Lancaster carrying the new ordnance, so the first raid had to be staged from Russsia. On 15 September Lancasters of 9 and 617 Squadrons took off, twenty carrying Tallboys, while seven carried mines. The attack was detected before the bombers arrived over the fjord and smoke

AIR ATTACKS ON *TIRPITZ*

Date	Location	Attacking Force	Damage to *Tirpitz*	Aircraft losses
8/9 January 1941	Wilhelmshaven	32 bombers	none	
15 January 1941	Wilhelmshaven	96 bombers	none	
16 January 1941	Wilhelmshaven	81 bombers	none	
29/30 January 1941	Wilhelmshaven	34 (25 Wellingtons, 9 Hampdens)	none	
1 March 1941	Wilhelmshaven	116 (Blenheims, Hampdens, Wellingtons, Whitleys)	none	one
28/29 May 1941	Kiel	14 Whitleys	none	one
20/21 June 1941	Kiel	115 (47 Wellingtons, 24 Hampdens, 20 Whitleys, 12 Stirlings, 11 Halifaxes)	none	two
7 September 1941	Kiel	?	none	two
29/30 January 1942	Faettenfjord, Norway	16 (7 Stirlings, 9 Halifaxes)	none	one
9 March 1942	At sea	12 Albacores from *Victorious*	none	two
29/30 March 1942	Faettenfjord, Norway	38 (27 Halifaxes, 11 Lancasters)		
30/31 March 1942	Faettenfjord, Norway	34 Halifaxes		
27/28 April 1942	Faettenfjord, Norway	44 (32 Halifaxes, 12 Lancasters)		(10 total in attacks since 29/30 March)
28/29 April 1942	Faettenfjord, Norway	23 Halifaxes		two
10 February 1944	Altafjord, Norway	15 Soviet bombers	none	
3 April 1944	Kaafjord, Norway	21 Barracudas 1st wave, 19 Barracudas 2nd wave, plus 40 fighters	severe	four
24 April 1944	Altafjord, Norway	cancelled	none	
15 May 1944	Altafjord, Norway	27 Barracudas from *Victorious* & *Furious*	none	
28 May 1944	Altafjord, Norway	cancelled	none	
17 July 1944	Kaafjord, Norway	45 Barracudas from *Furious* & *Formidable*	none	two
22 August 1944	Kaafjord, Norway	? 5 carriers	minor	
24 August 1944	Kaafjord, Norway	? 5 carriers	none	
29 August 1944	Kaafjord, Norway	? 5 carriers	none	
15 September 1944	Kaafjord, Norway	27 Lancasters	heavy bow damage	
18 October 1944	Tromso, Norway	7 Fireflies from *Implacable*	none	
29 October 1944	Tromso, Norway	19 Lancasters	moderate	
12 November 1944	Tromso, Norway	32 Lancasters	sunk	

A direct hit on *Tirpitz* during the air attack of 3 April 1944. Operation Tungsten employed 40 Barracuda dive bombers and 40 escorting fighters from the fleet carriers *Victorious* and *Furious* and four escort carriers. The raid caught the *Tirpitz* unprepared and fourteen direct hits did considerable damage.

This close-up view of the *Tirpitz* superstructure is from July 1942 when the ship was based in Faettenfjord. From June to July *Tirpitz* wore a very busy, multi-coloured camouflage scheme while based here. Later in July the *Tirpitz* moved to Bogenfjord near Narvik and received her first bar or ray camouflage scheme.

generators quickly obscured the target. Seventeen of the Tallboys were dropped but only one hit the ship. Nonetheless this one bomb proved the power of the new weapon. It passed through the bow of *Tirpitz* and detonated on the floor of the fjord. The pressure wave it generated tore a 55ft by 35ft hole in the lower hull and the entire bow of the ship from Anton barbette to the cutwater suffered severe structural damage. The forecastle was warped, fuel tanks were cracked, machinery was knocked off the mounts and forward compartments were flooded. Although it was not evident to British reconnaissance, this one hit basically ended the operational career of *Tirpitz*. With the extensive bow damage, she could not safely exceed 10kts in speed.

Tirpitz could not be adequately repaired in Norway so her career as flagship of Kampfgruppe 1 ended and Rear Admiral Peters lowered his flag. The hull received a temporary patch and on 16 October the *Tirpitz* put to sea for the last time. She limped northward at 8kts until she reached Tromso, where she anchored in shallow water next to Haakoy Island. Since the Admiralty still considered the *Tirpitz* fully functional, a new strike was planned, using specially stripped-down Lancasters which could just reach Tromso from a base in Scotland. On 29 October nineteen Lancasters bombed through breaks in the low cloud cover, and although there were no direct hits, several bombs landed close enough to *Tirpitz* to further damage the battleship.

Still lacking visual confirmation, the British decided to have another go at the *Tirpitz*. On 12 November 1944 thirty-two Lancasters of 9 and 617 Squadrons headed across the North Sea in Operation Catechism. Weather was good and the bombing accuracy was spectacular. Hits were registered on the forecastle, quarterdeck, aft of the stack, catapult, bridge, Bruno turret, starboard hull side as well as several near misses. The *Tirpitz* was shattered but, for the moment, still afloat. However, twenty minutes after the attack the magazine for Caesar turret exploded, blowing a huge 117ft hole below the waterline, and in a matter of minutes *Tirpitz* was listing at 40 degrees to port. 'Abandon ship' was ordered, and in another two minutes the list reached 70 degrees; she hit the shallow fjord bottom as she was still turning over.

At long last the threat was removed. The hulk was gradually dismembered after the war.

The *Tirpitz* on 30 March 1944. This shows her striking bar or ray type camouflage scheme. The ray patterns on the hull and superstructure were in dark grey and dark green.

Model Products

When models of warships in injected plastic began to appear in the 1950s the producers tended to favour kits of their own nation's warships, USN for Revell, RN for Airfix, and later the IJN for the Japanese manufacturers. However, there was no manufacturer in Germany who produced kits of the warships of the Third Reich. There were two notable exceptions to this trend in the 1950s: the Ideal Toy Company (ITC) produced a large scale *Graf Spee* and the New York company of Aurora pioneered their philosophy of producing models of warships of other countries with their *Graf Spee* in 1958. However, there was still no *Bismarck*. About the same time that the British movie *Sink the Bismarck* was released, a series of 1:1200 scale plastic kits made their appearance, first in the United Kingdom under the Eaglewall brand and then subsequently in the US under the Pyro label. These diminutive kits had British, US, German and Japanese subjects, including the *Bismarck*. Too small to satisfy many modellers, something bigger was needed and in 1962 Aurora released the first mid-size *Bismarck* kit. The race was on, and in a space of a few years almost every major model company across the world produced their own version, along with her sister-ship *Tirpitz*. However, with the appearance of the Aoshima *Bismarck/Tirpitz* in 1:700 scale and Tamiya *Bismarck/Tirpitz* in 1:350 scale, new kits on these subjects seemed to dry up. Decades were to pass before, suddenly, with a new century a new wave of fresh *Bismarck* models appeared. Three new 1:700 scale *Bismarck/Tirpitz* kits came out almost simultaneously, each one of which was infinitely superior to the earlier kits. As this is being written at the start of 2008 a new 1:350 scale model of the *Bismarck* is being produced by Revell of Germany, which promises to become the new standard in that scale, supplanting the older Tamiya kit.

Collectors' or Wargamers' Scales 1:1200, 1:1250 and 1:2400

Models of warships in 1:1200 or 1:1250 scales were first made commercially before World War Two, and similar naval recognition models were mass-produced during the conflict. Lacking detail by modern standards, these models are essentially collectors' items. A more recent offshoot is the even smaller 1:2400 scale, which allows wargaming at realistic scale ranges without the need of a gymnasium.

NEPTUN/NAVIS — 1:1250 Scale

The most prominent European manufacturer of metal models of warships is the German firm of Neptun/Navis. Neptun actually produces three different versions of *Bismarck* and *Tirpitz*: a basic version painted in overall light grey; the intermediate series presents the same models painted in camouflage schemes; while the top-end versions include camouflage plus rigging and display case. Shown here is the Neptun intermediate version of the *Bismarck* sporting her Baltic late trials camouflage scheme. The intermediate Neptun *Tirpitz* features a version of the splinter camouflage schemes worn by the Queen of the North. The details on these small models are outstanding and are only enhanced by the excellent and well-executed paint scheme.

■ Sample: **Courtesy of Collectio Navalis**
www.collnav.de

SUPERIOR 1:1200 Scale

A lineal descendant of World War Two USN recognition models, Superior produces both *Bismarck* and *Tirpitz* in white metal in 1:1200. Noticeably larger than the Navis models, the Superior ships come unpainted and with a small number of parts to be attached. These models have been consistently upgraded in detail over time but the Superior *Bismarck* and *Tirpitz* do not have the detail of the German products. They are solid and sturdy and optimised for wargamers. A very big plus for the Superior line is their cost, which is not much more than one-third the price of the version from Neptun.

The two models do reflect the differences between the two ships. The *Tirpitz* model does have the shelter deck at the catapult extending to the side of the hull and triple torpedo tubes on each side, different radar fit, different deck fittings arrangement and enhanced anti-aircraft gun ensemble.

■ Samples: **Courtesy of Alnavco** www.alnavco.com

REVELL *TIRPITZ* 1:1200 Scale

This kit is a throwback on more than one plane. This waterline plastic kit produced in 1:1200 scale by Revell in their Miniships range brings back memories of the first plastic kits of *Bismarck* and *Tirpitz* by Eaglewall and Pyro in this scale that appeared around 1961. It has one strong point – price. At around $5US it is the cheapest of the *Bismarck* kits. The box top states that it is the *Tirpitz* but the kit lacks the extended shelter deck and additional AA, so it appears that it is their version of the *Bismarck*, repackaged under new box art, except for the inclusion of torpedo tubes moulded onto the deck. The kit has separate hull and deck pieces plus 29 additional parts. Surprisingly, the kit includes two Arado seaplanes, which with their dark green camouflage scheme will add extra colour to the finished model. Keep the box as the building instructions are on the back. This is indeed a throwback to the detail and composition of kits of 40 years ago, and is only suitable for novice modellers.

■ Sample: **Courtesy of Freetime Hobbies** www.freetimehobbies.com

SUPERIOR 1:2400 Scale

In addition to their 1:1200 scale models, Superior/Alnavco also produces a line of smaller white metal warships in 1:2400 scale, including *Bismarck* and *Tirpitz*. This line has three significant positives: they are far less expensive than any other metal model, their small size allows easy storage of entire fleets, and at this scale detail is significantly reduced. The *Tirpitz* model does have the most significant differences, which distinguished her from *Bismarck*. This includes additional AA guns on Bruno turret, on the forward bridge and on the stack platform; enlarged shelter deck with crane mounted on shelter deck; and torpedo tubes. Separate turrets come four to a runner with two with AA mount and two without. For the *Bismarck* model two turret runners are included to provide four turrets without the AA.

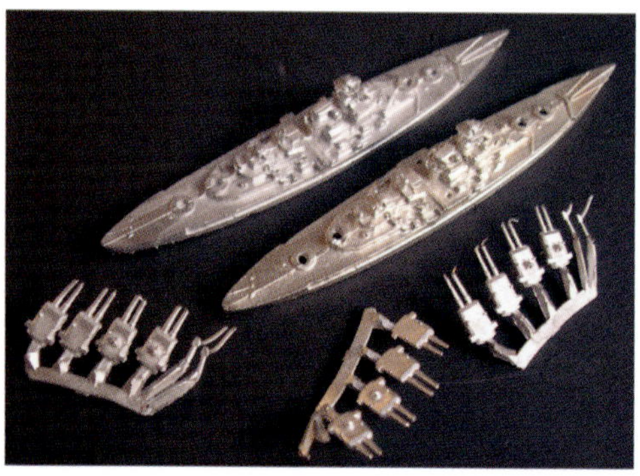

■ Samples: **Courtesy of Alnavco** www.alnavco.com

GHQ 1:2400 Scale

GHQ present an alternative in the Lilliputian scale of 1:2400. For their small size, these are really nice models. As with the Superior models, they come unpainted. However, they require more assembly than their Superior 1:2400 cousins. Superstructures, masts, turrets, cranes and other items must be attached to the hull. The GHQ products have significantly greater detail but come at a significantly higher price. Each model comes with a hull piece, superstructure piece, six runners of smaller parts and a rudimentary set of assembly instructions sufficient for the purpose and size of the model. As with the Superior models in this scale, the GHQ shows the same differences between *Bismarck* and *Tirpitz*, but the *Tirpitz* model has additional light AA mounts omitted in the Superior version.

Samples: **Courtesy of Alnavco** www.alnavco.com

Mid-size Scales 1:570 to 1:803 Scale

This is the battleground for commercial *Bismarck*/*Tirpitz* kits – more kits by far have been produced in the mid-size arena than in the smaller and larger sizes combined. After the flurry of competing *Bismarck* kits in the 1960s in 1:600 and 1:570 scales, culminating in the first 1:700 scale waterline *Bismarck* in the early 1970s, there was a hiatus until the advent of the 21st century brought new *Bismarck* and *Tirpitz* kits, first highly detailed and expensive resin kits from the Czech Republic, then highly detailed injected plastic kits from Japan and China.

AURORA *BISMARCK* 1:600 Scale

Can you remember a time when the box art of a model made an indelible impression upon you, an experience so memorable that it stayed with you for decades thereafter? Box art sells models, and Aurora knew it. The *Bismarck* box art was the most gloriously excessive example of an alluring image – and it didn't matter that the ship never wore the camouflage scheme portrayed. It was a classic example of sizzle over substance.

This kit was released years before the four-company Japanese consortium popularised the 1:700 scale waterline format, but in some respects this Aurora kit is a linear ancestor. First of all it is in a standard scale, as 1:600 was the standard for Aurora kits. Secondly, it is the first larger kit that had waterline construction as an option, whereby the upper hull slid inside the lower hull. The kit designed apparently tried to create the effect of an armour belt at this juncture, but the hull sides were so thick that the armour belt appears to scale out at least 6ft in width. Unlike other kits the seams of the deck planks were incised and not raised, but they are so deep that you could run trolleys along the deck. Typical of the time, the kit featured solid thick railing but then so did Revell and Renwal kits. Nor were Aurora designers ever very exacting in duplicating secondary and tertiary armament: muzzles ended in flash and resemble the ends of Q-tips or reversed Dahlgrens. Clearly, if you are looking for fidelity or detail, give the Aurora *Bismarck* a wide berth. Furthermore, one of the current 1:700 *Bismarck* kits, in addition to being a far better kit than the Aurora *Bismarck*, will probably be significantly cheaper than the price that you'll have to pay on the collector's market for this out of production kit.

Sample: **Author's Collection**

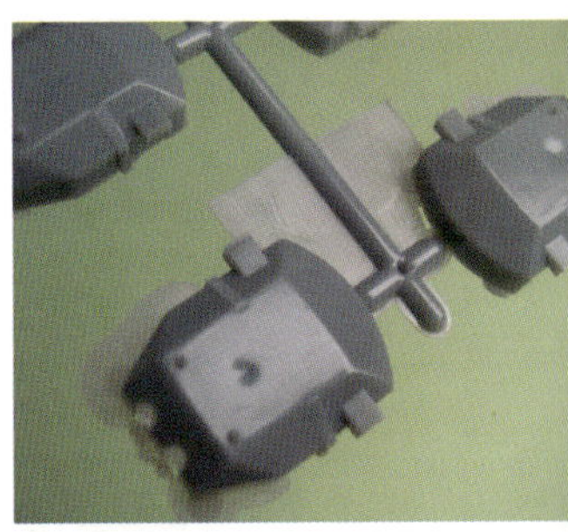

AIRFIX *BISMARCK* — 1:600 Scale

Shortly after Aurora produced the first first mid-size *Bismarck* kit, across the Atlantic Airfix produced another in 1:600, a natural companion to its existing HMS *Hood* kit. For this British firm it was its first venture into 'foreign' warship subjects, and its commercial success led to models of other well-known adversaries of the Royal Navy, notably *Graf Spee*, *Prinz Eugen* and *Scharnhorst*. The Airfix *Bismarck* is still in production, and having long since paid off its development costs, it is one of the least expensive plastic kits of the battleship currently available.

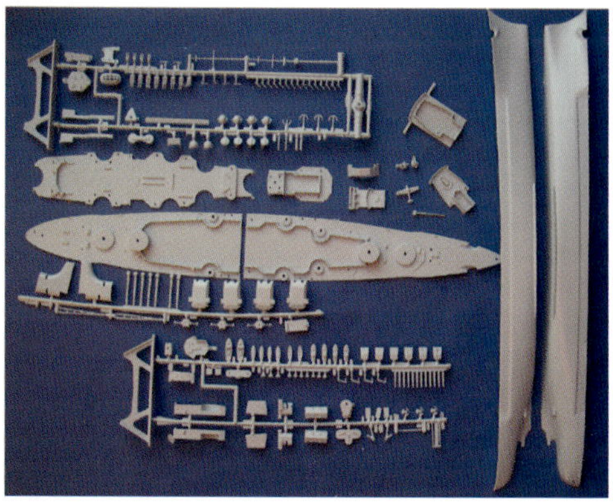

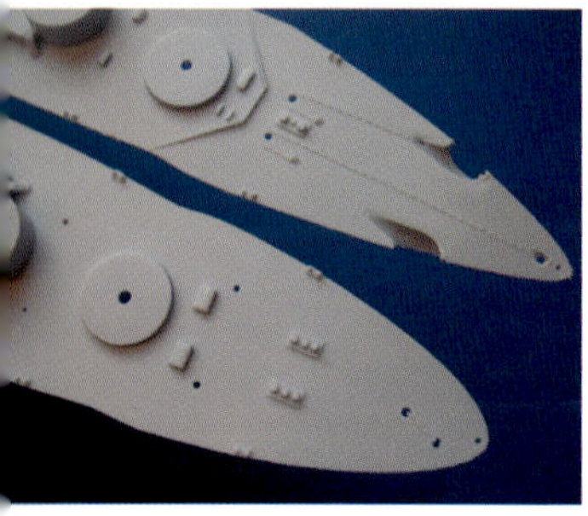

The *Bismarck* is produced in the standard Airfix format with a full hull divided along the centreline. The hull halves have a minimal amount of detail with oversize portholes indicated by raised circles, but does show the projecting armour belt, bilge keels and propeller shaft shrouds. There is a stern anchor on the port side but does not provide for the recessed area where the anchor was actually stowed, but the bow hawse arrangements are better. The deck pieces exhibit detail typical of other Airfix kits of the time. Decent deck planking detail is indicated by raised lines at the seams, rather than incised lines. There is a low to moderate level of deck fittings, anchor chains and twin bollard fittings. The kit does come with the solid, triangular shaped 'Aztec steps' to represent inclined ladders, so typical of almost every plastic ship of the time, but now rendered archaic by fine photo-etch products. Overall shapes are good, even if detail is somewhat sparse and Airfix was ahead of its time in including individual 20mm AA guns. The box art portrays the *Bismarck* at the time of her loss, with turret crowns painted yellow. Today the Airfix kit still provides good value to anyone wanting a full hull version of the ship, and one that is readily capable of being upgraded with photo-etch after-market sets, all at a fraction of the costs of any of the newest 1:700 scale waterline kits.

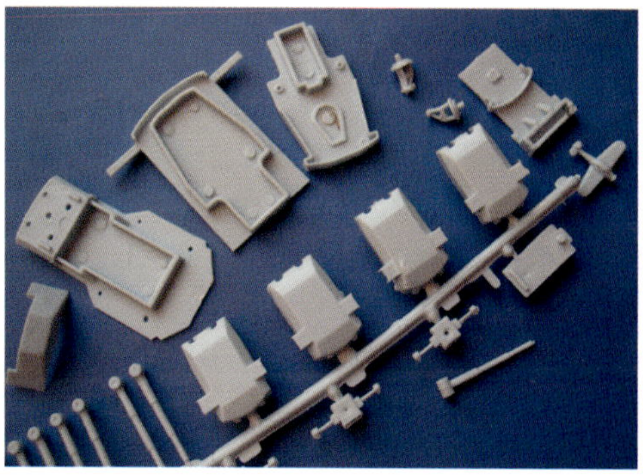

Sample: **Courtesy of Freetime Hobbies**
www.freetimehobbies.com

REVELL *BISMARCK* — 1:570 Scale

The third entrant into the 1960s *Bismarck* race came from the California firm of Revell. One of the earliest producers of injected plastic kits, Revell had started producing warship kits in 1951 with the *Iowa* class battleships. Like Airfix, for more than a decade Revell had stuck with producing plastic kits of 'home' subjects, but in 1964 they produced their first non-USN ship and that was of course the German *Bismarck*. They also produced it in a non-standard scale with 1:570 being chosen, apparently, to increase the size of the model over competing kits from Aurora and Airfix. Considering that this kit was designed over forty years ago, it still has a very creditable level of detail and was the best of the first wave of *Bismarck* kits in the 1960s. The box art is dramatic but inaccurate, as it shows her attacked by Swordfish while still wearing her Baltic camouflage stripes, which were over-painted before her Atlantic sortie.

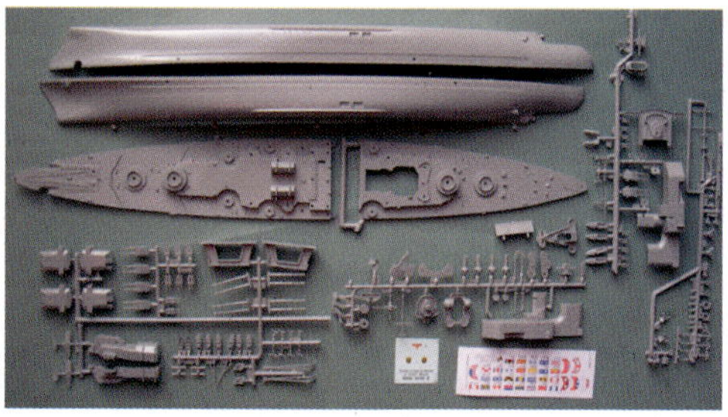

The raised crest shields on either side of the bow on the model are also wrong, as they were removed before combat operations. Outmoded features of the hull include the solid deck edge railing, and the raised waterline, but the Revell *Bismarck* has detail on the hull not found in the kits from Aurora or Airfix. In addition to bilge keels, the kit has a remarkable level of detail to the lower hull, although there is a question about accuracy. The *Bismarck* kit has two recessed louvered vents on each side above the aft bilge keel, but the shape appears to be incorrect and the positions too few in number for *Bismarck*. The hull fairings added with the Atlantik bow are present, while the deck shows the same raised seam lines for deck planking and 'Aztec steps' found in the Airfix kit. The breakwaters are too thick but considering that this kit is over forty years old there is a surprising amount of detail – like cable reels – made part of the deck. Superstructure parts include ventilation louvres, portholes, doors and vertical ladder. There are nicely done ship's boats and individual 20mm guns, but they are not quite as fine as the the Airfix ones. The Revell *Bismarck* has held up well and is one of the lower priced *Bismarck* kits on the market. It presents a slightly greater level of detail than the Airfix kit but some of this detail is inaccurate. The odd scale can also pose a problem when it comes to adding photo-etch parts.

Sample: **Courtesy of Freetime Hobbies**
www.freetimehobbies.com

REVELL ***TIRPITZ*** 1:570 Scale

Revell had a decade-old tradition of repackaging old kits in new boxes under names of various sister-ships. Growing up, I had the Revell *Bismarck* when it was released but never did get the Revell *Tirpitz* because the dramatic artwork on the box cover, with *Tirpitz* in a Norwegian Fjord under air attack, showed the ship wearing the Baltic trial stripes of *Bismarck* not a *Tirpitz* scheme. Therefore, I expected to find a model identical to their *Bismarck* kit. I was wrong. Revell indeed includes separate parts with this *Tirpitz* kit to recreate the appearance differences between the two ships. It is essentially the same kit as their *Bismarck*, but one of the sprues has been enlarged to include additional parts – a *Tirpitz* name plate, additional AA positions, Bruno turret, stack cap, HA directors and, most importantly, additional cut-outs to extend the shelter deck to the hull sides as found on *Tirpitz*. I was very impressed that that the designers of this old kit made a very credible effort in presenting the differences between the two ships, which may be the first time this was ever attempted in the plastic industry.

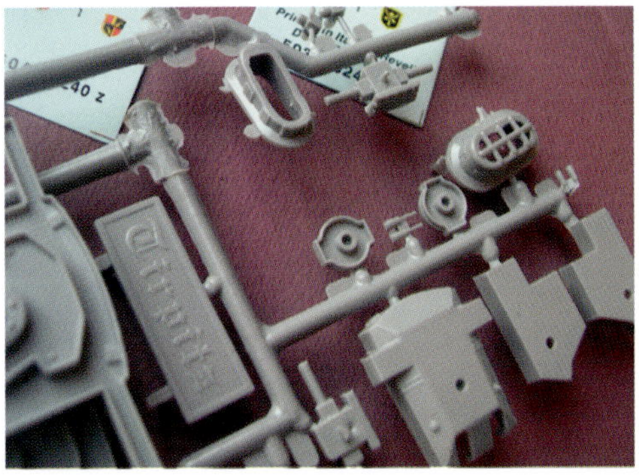

Sample: **Courtesy of Freetime Hobbies**
www.freetimehobbies.com

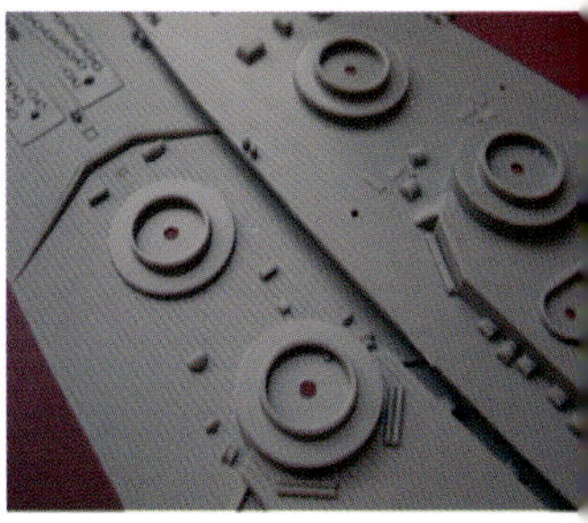

MINIHOBBYMODELS ***TIRPITZ*** 30CM Scale

MiniHobbyModels has a series entitled 30CM scale in which each kit is 300mm long, whether it is a destroyer or battleship. Since the *Bismarck* and *Tirpitz* were 248m in length, the kit is approximately in 1:803 scale, although the size of the box suggest something far larger. A separate sticker on the box top states 'static model' to differentiate it from the original release of the kit, which included a small battery-powered electric motor. However, even the static version is not much better than a bath toy, with no detail on the hull sides, and inaccurate or over-scale fittings – anchors stowed on the fore-castle, for example, and hawse channels omitted altogether. The superstructure parts lack any porthole or door detail, and the catapult is wrongly positioned and scales out to be about seven feet high. There are many other shortcomings, but the kit is not worth a detailed critique. Although produced in 2001, it makes the 45-year old Aurora *Bismarck* seem like perfection incarnate

Sample: **Courtesy of Freetime Hobbies**
www.freetimehobbies.com

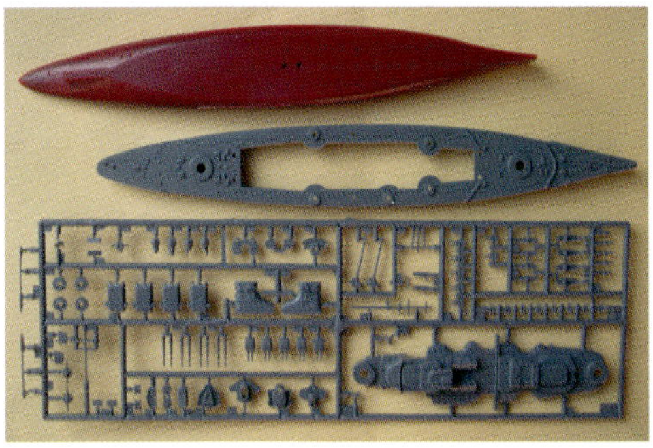

SAMEK *BISMARCK* — 1:700 Scale

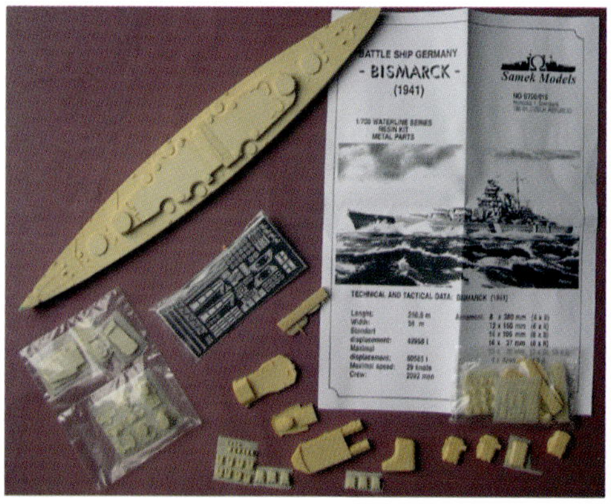

The last quarter of the twentieth century was a period of rapid developments in kit production techniques, yet there had been no new *Bismarck* or *Tirpitz* models since the lacklustre Aoshima 1:700 scale releases in the 1970s. It is a truism that resin kits cannot compete against injected plastic kits on account of price, because although resin can carry far greater detail than injected plastic, resin kits are hand-produced in hundreds rather than mass-manufactured in tens of thousands. With the appearance of a plastic kit of even remotely equivalent detail, the resin kit will cease production because the plastic kit can be sold at one-quarter to one-fifth the price of the resin kit. However, with the *Bismarck* and *Tirpitz* there was a void and Samek of the Czech Republic stepped in to produce state of the art kits for both *Bismarck* and *Tirpitz* in waterline 1:700 scale. The window was only opened for a short period of time for within a few years not one, but three new plastic kits of both *Bismarck* and *Tirpitz* appeared from Japan and China, ending production of this much more expensive resin kit.

When the Samek *Bismarck* and *Tirpitz* kits appeared, they were a quantum leap superior to the original Aoshima *Bismarck*. The hull casting still has the best deck planking detail of any *Bismarck* kit to date with plank butt-end detail. The first level of the superstructure is cast integral with the hull and has excellent side detail, especially with the ventilators clustered around the barbettes of Bruno and Caesar turrets. Splinter shields and breakwaters have far greater fineness than even later plastic kits, although the breakwaters lack support brackets. Hull sides have good detail with scuttles, armour belt and boat booms, but lack the recess for the stern anchor and main anchors outboard fairings. Superstructure and smaller parts detail is good but has been eclipsed by all three subsequent injected plastic kits. The kits came with a small steel photo-etch fret produced by Eduard also of the Czech Republic. With the coming of the new plastic kits, production of the Samek kits ceased and now are normally only found for sale on auction sites.

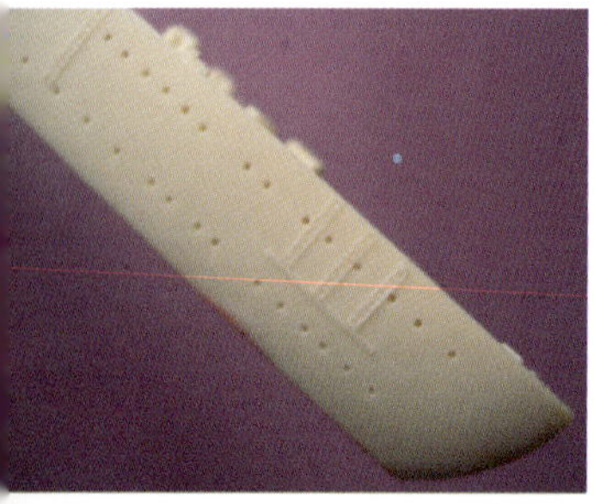

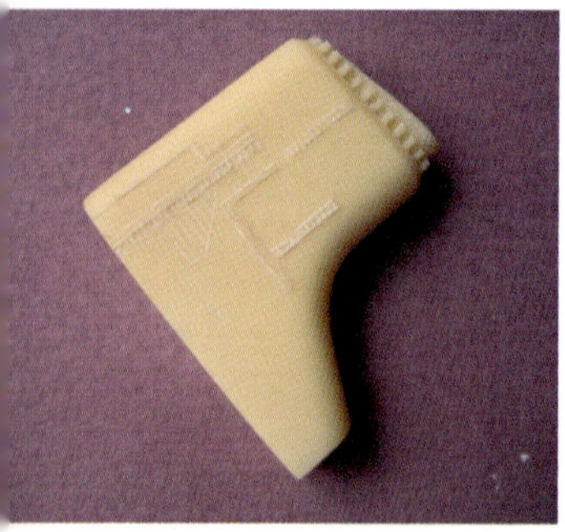

Sample: **Courtesy of David Lilly**

AOSHIMA *BISMARCK* — 1:700 Scale New Mouldings

In the early 1970s four Japanese plastic model companies formed a cartel with the extraordinarily ambitious plan of establishing a universal and constant scale line of warship model kits. The various subjects were divided among the four companies, Tamiya, Hasegawa, Aoshima and Fujimi, and the huge output of kits made 1:700 scale waterline by far the most popular of all formats. Aoshima had the *Bismarck/Tirpitz* concession in the cartel and produced 1:700 scale kits of both ships in the early 1970s. However, these kits were bland in the extreme, as they were the basic models with no frills. No other plastic kit manufacturer wanted to go up against the cartel with the lone exception of Matchbox, which did produce a limited line of 1:700 scale waterline kits, but not the *Bismarck* or *Tirpitz*. However, the cartel fell apart in the 1990s, so without the protection of a monopoly the drab offerings from Aoshima were open to competition.

Whether it was the appearance of the resin Samek kit or rumours of injected plastic kits of the *Bismarck* pair coming from China, Aoshima roused themselves to

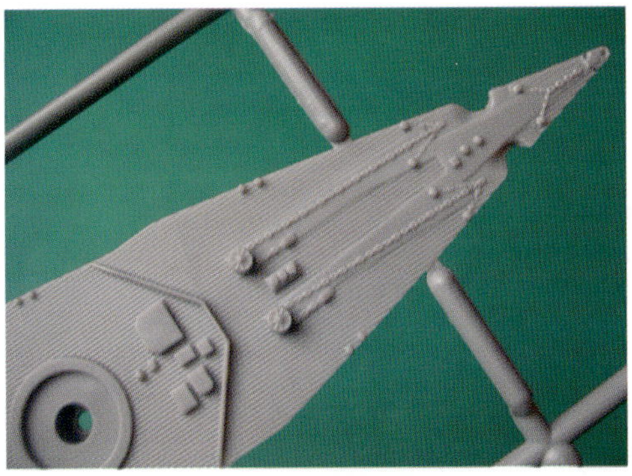

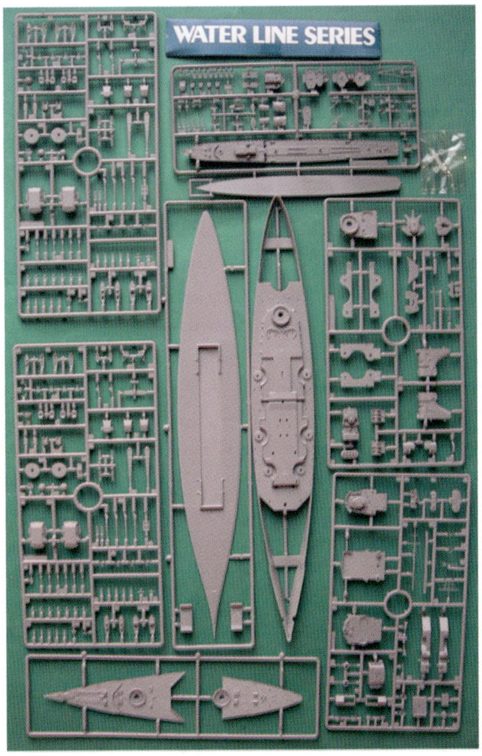

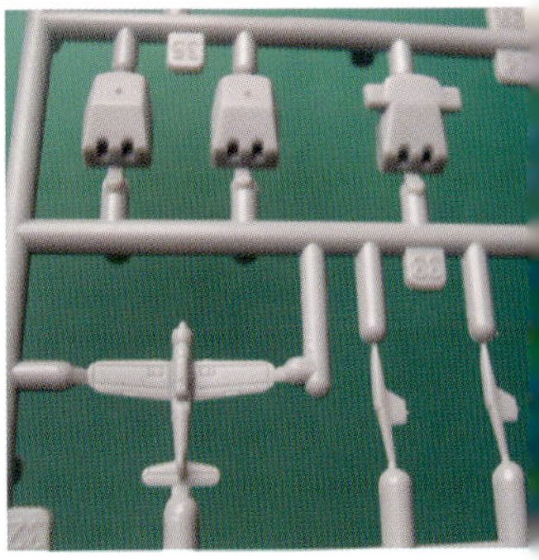

produce a new and thoroughly modernised version of *Bismarck*, which is far superior to their first version. It is far better detailed but still misses some significant design features. The one-piece waterline hull has nice lines with good porthole and armoured belt detail. Although it has the recess for the stern anchor, it omits the outboard fairings for the main anchors and completely misses the bow anchor at the top of the cutwater, except for the anchor chain on the deck, which leads to nothing. There is a very nice level of deck detail, and on many of the smaller parts, especially the stack halves, with support bracing underneath various platforms, and ventilation louvre, door and porthole detail on superstructure parts. As a sweetener, Aoshima throws in an additional kit, a complete 1:700 scale waterline model of a German destroyer, the *Z23*. Although a very good effort, the new-tooled Aoshima *Bismarck* kit is significantly more expensive than either of the new kits produced by either of the two Chinese companies.

Sample: **Courtesy of Freetime Hobbies**
www.freetimehobbies.com

DRAGON *TIRPITZ* 1:700 Scale

In addition to Aoshima, two Chinese kit producers were in the race to release new design *Bismarck* kits – Dragon Models Limited (DML), based in Hong Kong and long-established; and arch-rival Trumpeter, a new firm from mainland China. In 2004 Dragon released its versions of *Bismarck* and *Tirpitz*. Of all of the injected plastic kits of the ships, only the Dragon offerings include a brass photo-etch fret as standard. The much more expensive resin Samek kit does have photo-etch but the Dragon fret is superior. Although the Dragon kit is based on the standard 1:700 scale waterline hull, DML wandered off the reservation by also including lower hull parts, the full-hull option being a rarity in 1:700 scale. Unlike the Aoshima kit, Dragon does have the bow anchor fairings as well as the stern recess. The fairing on the *Tirpitz* is of a horseshoe shape, rather than a crescent design found

on the DML *Bismarck* kit. Dragon is really to be congratulated for picking up on this small variance between the two ships. However, my sample of the *Tirpitz* kit did have a blemish on the hull side. Although portholes are found at both sides of the stern and on the starboard side of the bow, they don't appear on the port bow. This appears to be an aberration with this particular kit, as the Dragon *Bismarck* kit has the correct portholes on each side of the hull.

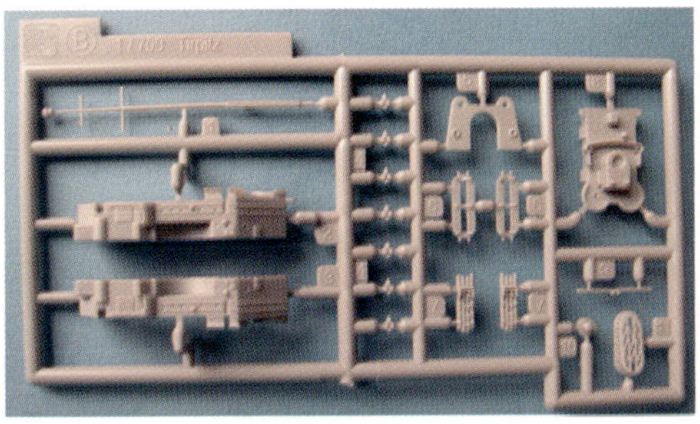

Hallelujah! Someone finally has produced a *Bismarck*/*Tirpitz* kit with support brackets for the breakwaters, and the excellent detail of the deck pieces continues with fine planking, hose reels and deck coamings. The shelter deck is a separate piece, which is better than providing inserts to fill out the *Tirpitz* shelter deck as was done in the old Revell kit. The catapult moulding is solid but finely detailed, portrayed with the amid-

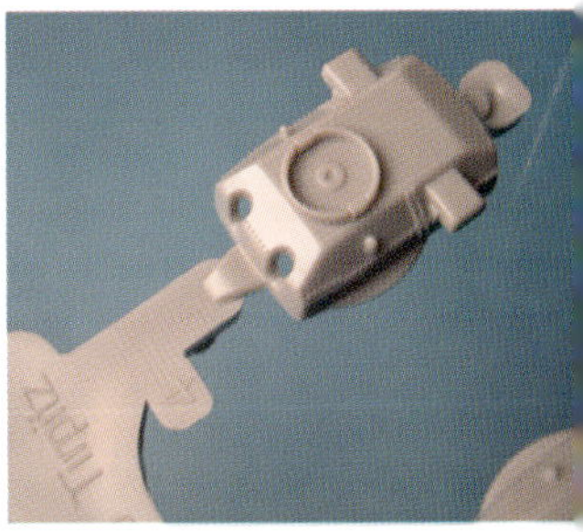

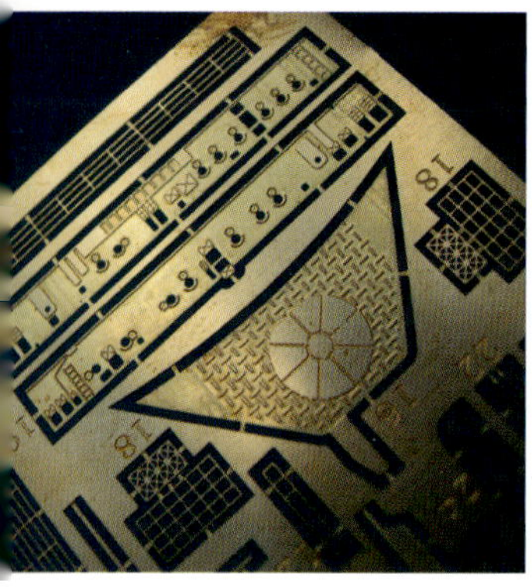

ships section covered by plates which were removed when the catapult was to be used. Superstructure detail includes high quality piping, ventilation louvres, doors and portholes. In their original *Bismarck* and *Tirpitz* kits, Dragon produced some parts of the superstructure in a hard rubber material, rather than with injected plastic, which were not well received in the modelling community. Other than being different in composition, I do not see any disadvantage to their use other than the need for 'super-glue' in lieu of traditional plastic model cement for their attachment. The Arados and ship's boats are in clear plastic, so the glass-work on these small miniatures will be clear. Dragon provides a great deal of value in this kit. With a high level of detail, brass photo-etch, and optional lower hull parts, it is an

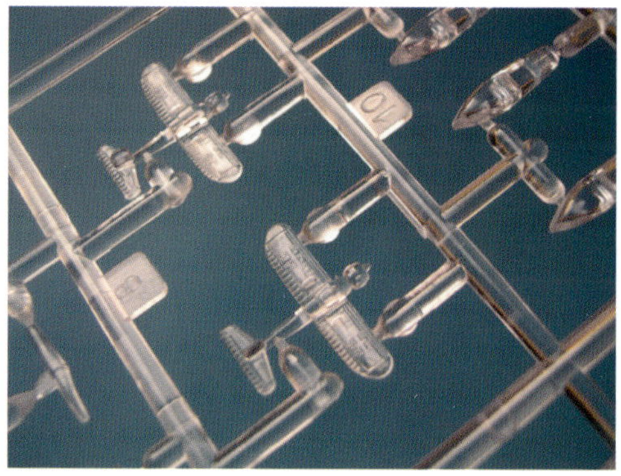

outstanding *Tirpitz* kit with greater detail and a lower price than the new-mould Aoshima release.

Sample: **Courtesy of Freetime Hobbies**
www.freetimehobbies.com

DRAGON ***BISMARCK*** 1:700 Scale Premium Edition

The usual Dragon sales strategy is to first produce a standard plastic kit and then subsequently release a deluxe edition as a 'Premium Edition', one key feature being the inclusion of a brass photo-etch fret providing for even finer details. However, the DML *Bismarck* and *Tirpitz* kits had the brass photo-etch fret included in the kits from their initial release, so what distinguishes the 2006 'Premium Edition' of their two-year old *Bismarck* kit? For the most part they both share identical parts laid out in identical sprues, but there are contrasts and variations. Dragon had listened to modellers' discontent with the original rubber parts, which in the Premium Edition DML replaced with traditional injected plastic

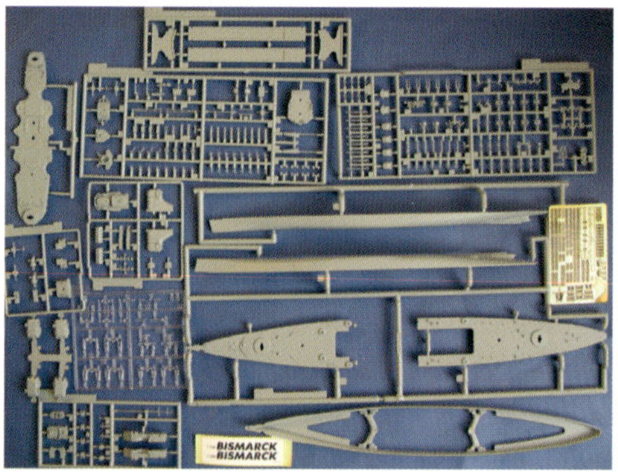

versions. Another addition is the expansion of the contents of the brass photo-etch fret, which uses all the very nice detail of the original – especially the spectacular superstructure sides with open portholes and deadlights (covers) – but reorganised it to include cable/hose reels in three different styles, anchors and finer radar arrays. The Dragon *Bismarck* kit fine-tunes the already excellent standard DML release.

Sample: **Courtesy of Dragon Models Limited**
www.dragonmodelsusa.com

TRUMPETER ***TIRPITZ*** 1:700 Scale

The year 2004 saw the introduction of another *Bismarck*/*Tirpitz* pair from a relatively new Chinese company, Trumpeter of Guangdong. They started with some kits in odd scales on Chinese navy subjects but

then joined the mainstream with kits of other countries' warships. Although still subject to design problems, Trumpeter has made consistent improvements to the quality of their kits. With the Trumpeter 1:700 scale *Tirpitz*, the leap in quality is obvious. The Trumpeter kits go head to head with the Dragon versions, as both companies released their kits the same year. However, Trumpeter made different design decisions, with a full hull option provided by a red one-piece lower hull and a separate red base plate for a waterline version. Unlike DML, Trumpeter provides exactly the same hull piece for both

Bismarck and *Tirpitz*, missing the slight variance found in the Dragon kits. Trumpeter includes the shelter deck as part of the hull and therefore also identical, extra inserts to enlarge the shelter deck of *Tirpitz* in an updated version of the Revell approach. This will create deck seams, which need to be filled, so I give the edge to the Dragon approach of providing separate and different shelter decks.

Trumpeter also provides excellent detail with support brackets for breakwaters and a wealth of fine deck fittings. At first glance the Trumpeter shelter deck bulkheads seem to lack detail, but Trumpeter supplies separate bulkhead parts to be applied. This provides superb detail on these structures but it does create extra seams to be filled. Other superstructure details on the Trumpeter kits are as good or perhaps better than found in the competing Dragon kits. Trumpeter clearly provides the best deck patterns, as not only are wooden plank

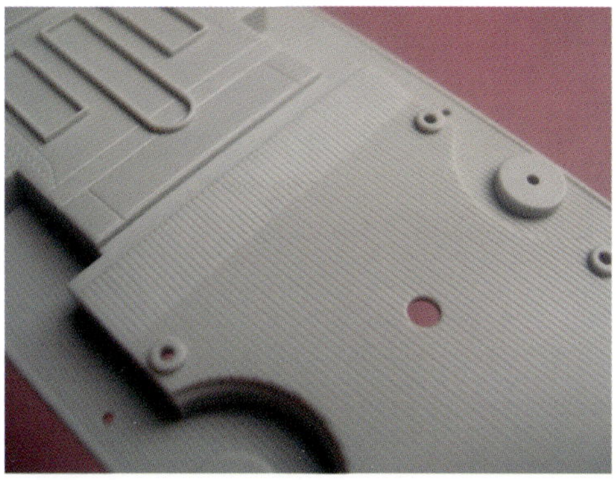

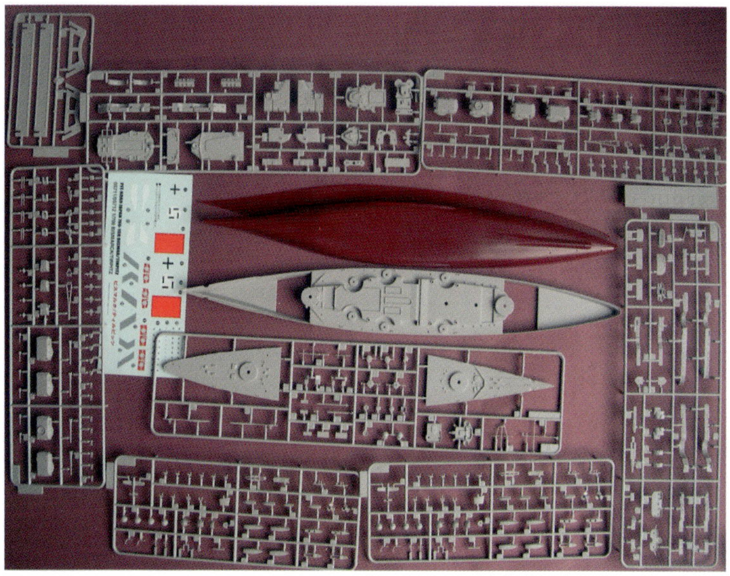

decks delineated but various metal anti-skid deck patterns are portrayed. At each level Trumpeter provides excellent parts and offers the unique option of allowing the catapult to be portrayed retracted or extended; two detailed grey plastic Arados are included. Turret detail is also fine with individual rivet detail on the main turrets Although Trumpeter includes a full decal sheet, as does Dragon, Trumpeter does not include any photo-etch. By any standard the Trumpeter *Tirpitz* is a splendid kit with its own strengths and weaknesses.

■ Sample: **Courtesy of Pacific Front**
www.pacificfront.com

SKY WAVE ***BISMARCK*** 1:700 Scale

This is marketed by a long established Japanese firm that used to produce three lines of kits. Pit-Road Hi-Mold was the brand for expensive resin kits of the highest quality; Waveline was the mark for moderately priced resin and some plastic kits, still with fine detail but not to the same exacting standards as the premium Hi-Mold kits; Sky Wave was the brand name for the lower priced injected plastic kits in competition with the likes of Tamiya, Hasegawa, Fujimi and Aoshima. Pit-Road seems to have entered into a working arrangement with Trumpeter of China. Very expensive resin kits produced in the Pit-Road Hi-Mold line

are beginning to appear in injected plastic from Trumpeter at far lower prices. Also part of this relationship is the apparent joint design of some kits with different distribution rights. Pit-Road retains distribution rights for any new joint design in the Japanese market while Trumpeter has distribution rights elsewhere. Such is the case with this Pit-Road Sky Wave 1:700 scale *Bismarck* kit. This is exactly the same kit as appears under the Trumpeter label but at a significantly higher price. You get new beautiful box art on the Sky Wave packaging but that's about it for differences. As the actual kit is identical to the Trumpeter version, it has the same strengths and weaknesses.

■ Sample: **Courtesy of Freetime Hobbies**
www.freetimehobbies.com

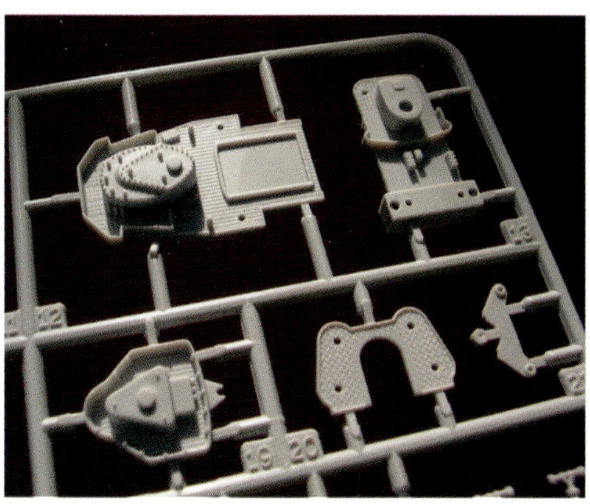

The Big Boys – 1:400 to 1:350 Scale

The *Bismarck* was a big ship and no small model can quite capture mass of this beautiful design like the kits in 1:400 or 1:350 scale. The American firm of Lindberg was first off the mark in the mid-1960s with a large *Bismarck* kit in allegedly 1:400 scale, but it was the French firm of Heller which popularised this scale and their kits of *Bismarck* and *Tirpitz* soon followed. However, the classic large *Bismarck*/*Tirpitz* model was produced by Tamiya in their 1:350 range, which has eight times the mass of the popular Japanese 1:700 scale line. However, Revell of Germany will have released their own new model of *Bismarck* in 1:350 scale before this volume is printed and this kit should replace the venerable Tamiya kits as best of the large models.

HELLER *BISMARCK* 1:400 Scale

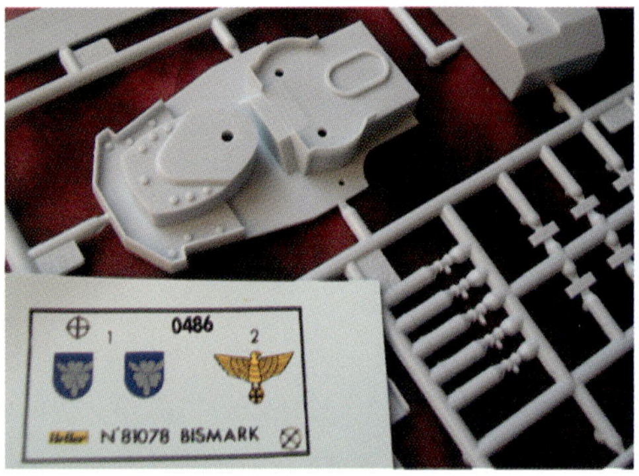

The Heller kit was originally produced in the late 1960s and was head and shoulders better than the Lindberg kit – and it is still in production. Unfortunately, my review sample was short of hull and deck pieces – the first time in many purchases of Heller kits that anything was missing – but although Heller offered to replace the parts, they wanted extra for shipping. However, I was not inclined to be double-dipped for parts that should have been included in the box from the start, so this review of the Heller *Bismarck* will be as truncated as the contents of the kit.

The detail was good for its time but is somewhat dated by today's standards. There are ventilation louvre details on the sides of the stack and a couple of superstructure pieces that include doors, circular porthole and square window detail, and a funnel cap with nice steam pipes and an open grid top screen. One advanced feature is the inclusion of separate breakwaters with support brackets. Additionally, the strut detail on the Arado floatplane is still pretty nice. Heller was also ahead of its time in having open lattice parts, such as cranes and railings, although a modern modeller probably would not use them in this era of extraordinarily fine photo-etch. Basic forms are there but detail is lacking, and on the whole, the Heller *Bismarck* presents a solid if somewhat dated model, at least as far as the parts I could examine.

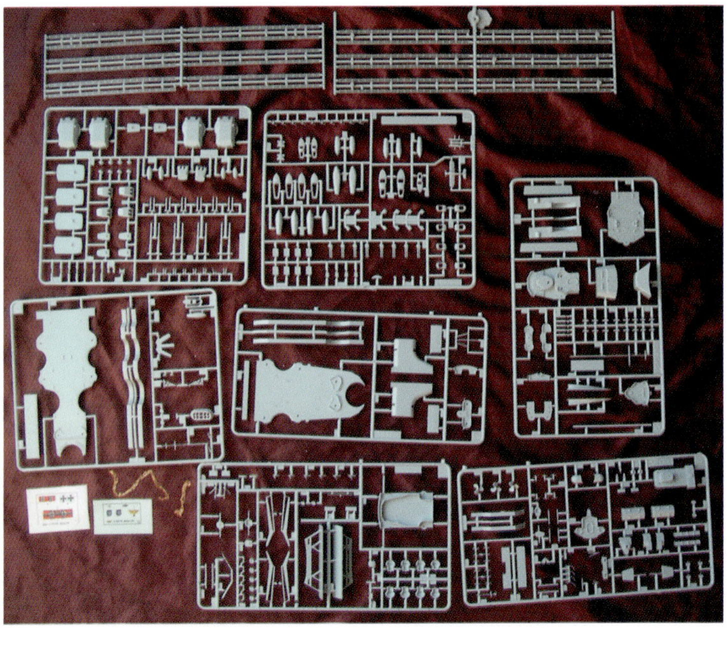

Sample: **Courtesy of Freetime Hobbies**
www.freetimehobbies.com

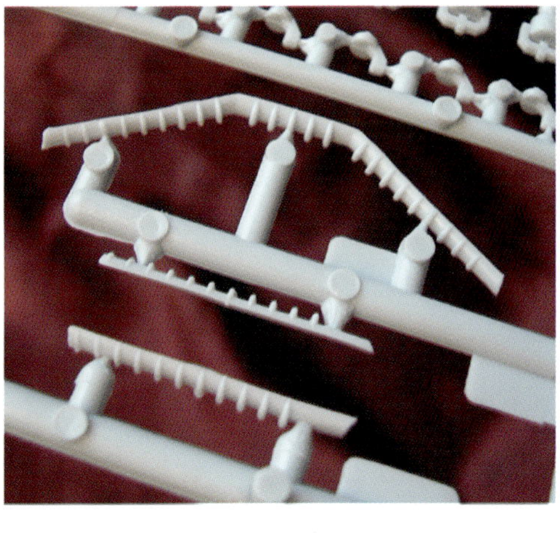

TAMIYA *TIRPITZ* 1:350 Scale

The Grand Dames of *Bismarck* and *Tirpitz* kits come from Tamiya in 1:350 scale, and have serenely ruled the world of large mass-produced models for a quarter of a century. Recently Tamiya put the pair under new box art and raised their price but it is still the same old kit underneath. The lower hull is a solid one-piece design and is equipped for a battery box and motorisation, but does not compromise the accuracy of the hull, as is sometimes found in smaller motorised kits. The hull detail is good with the recess for stern anchor, bow outboard anchor fairings, portholes, bilge keels, armour belt indentation and side climbing rungs. Unfortunately faint raised lines are found on the hull as guides for painting the boot-topping. The main deck comes in three parts with forecastle, amidships with shelter deck, and quarterdeck, with additional parts for the *Tirpitz* shelter deck extensions. As with any Tamiya kit, mouldings are crisp and clean. Deck detail is good but dated, and breakwaters do not have support brackets, which is a significant omission in this scale. On the forecastle there are slightly raised guidelines for painting the aerial recognition flag but not found at the quarterdeck position. Other than wooden deck planking for the main deck, none of the other deck textures are portrayed, so a valuable addition is the White Ensign Models brass relief-etched superstructure decking (in WEM PE 3565, reviewed below).

Superstructure parts are well made but the splinter shielding is too thick, as is common in injected plastic kits. Superstructure bulkheads have door, window and vertical ladder detail, but some ladders form thin right-angle pyramids which are best replaced with brass. Louvred vents are found on the superstructure and funnel sides. The funnel halves also have

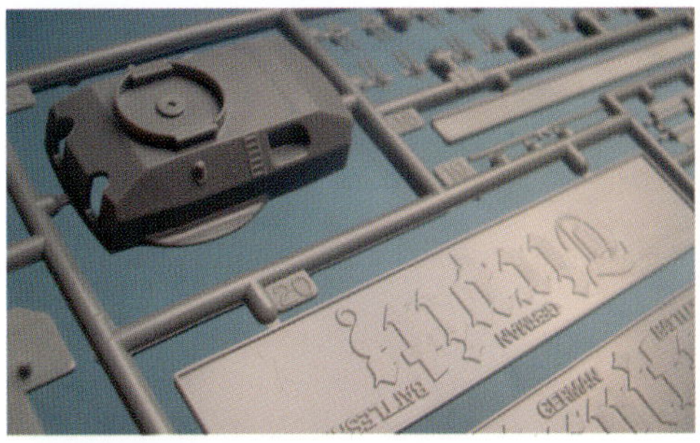

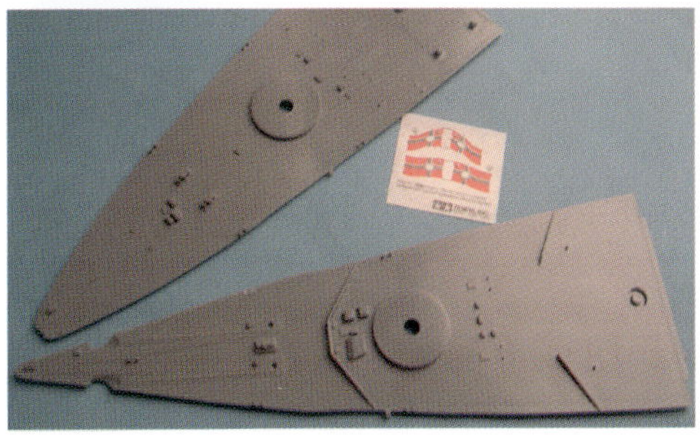

horizontal band detail but overdone vertical ladders. Very nice support detail is provided underneath platforms, and the main hangar door well captures the lattice grid pattern. Main gun turrets have base aprons, light rivet detail, vertical ladder and other fittings moulded onto them. Unfortunately, the funnel cap is solid, which just won't do in a model of this size, but it is easy to hollow it out and replace with brass funnel grating. The solid chunks of plastic that caricature the radar array should also be replaced with photo-etch. Two Arados are included but their design seems slightly off. For the *Tirpitz* kit Tamiya provides an additional plastic sprue with Bruno turret (without the deck tread pattern for the anti-aircraft gun position), torpedo tubes, shelter deck extensions, name plates, additional AA guns and assorted other parts. The Tamiya *Tirpitz* has ruled the waves for more than a generation, but it is certainly not state of the art.

Revell of Germany will have a new 1:350 scale model of *Bismarck* (and presumably *Tirpitz*) on sale in 2008. Will this new German release be a mere pretender to the throne or the true and rightful queen? Given the age of the Tamiya kit, odds favour the latter.

Sample: **Courtesy of Pacific Front**
www.pacificfront.com

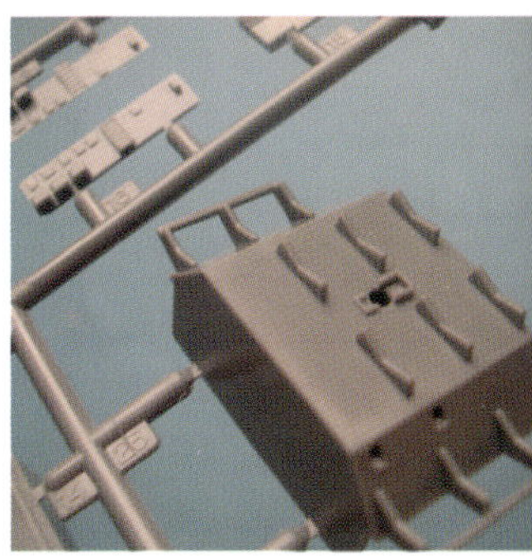

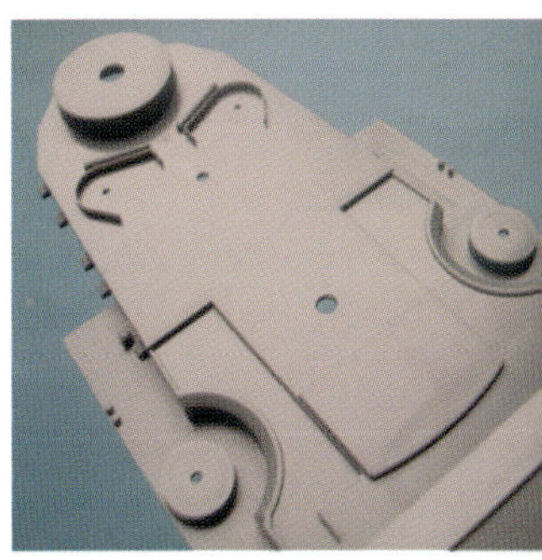

KANGNAM *TIRPITZ*

1:400 Scale

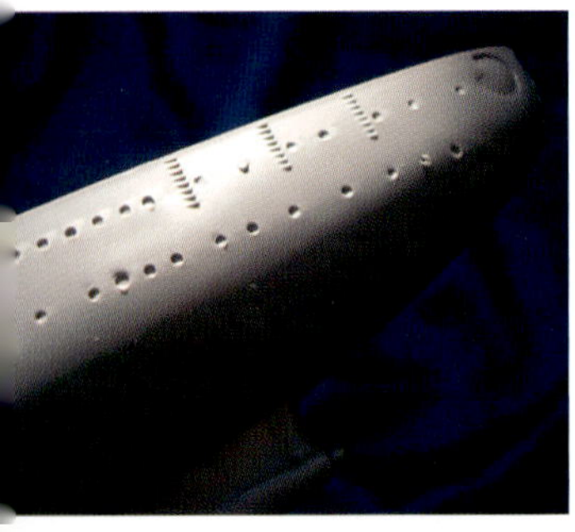

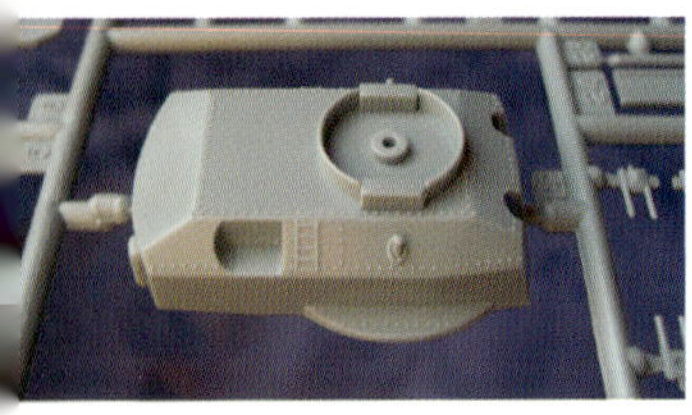

I had not heard of Kangnam and was expecting a down-sized poorly cloned version of the Tamiya *Tirpitz*. I was right in that it appears to be a pantographed version of the Tamiya kit produced in 1:400 scale, but I was wrong in anticipating poor quality parts. The Kangnam parts are, with some exceptions, good, but the Kangnam execution is not as crisp as the Tamiya kit, and the Chinese company missed on some details. Portholes are shallow and in a couple of porthole positions there are plastic nubs protruding from the hull. There are two significant errors on the Kangnam kit. The bow cutouts for the anchor positions, along with the outboard fairings are not present. The forecastle deck has the anchor channels so it is fairly easy to recreate the hull side cutouts but the fairings would need to be built up with some substance.

The deck planking is not quite of fine as the larger Tamiya models and in both cases seams are raised rather than incised. Beyond this, fitting for fitting the Kangnam decks match the Tamiya kit. Kangnam has organised the smaller parts on fewer sprues, and for the most part these are smaller replicas of Tamiya's, and just as crisp. However, there are notable exceptions where Kangnam fell on its collective face – the one Arado is terrible: dump it and get the resin 1:400 scale Arado produced by L'Arsenal of France. The ship's boats with Kangnam are far inferior to the Tamiya versions, but there are no ready-made substitutes for *Bismarck*/*Tirpitz* boats. Still, I prefer this kit to the Heller equivalent in this scale, probably because it is merely a slightly smaller version of the Tamiya kit.

Sample: **Courtesy of Freetime Hobbies**
www.freetimehobbies.com

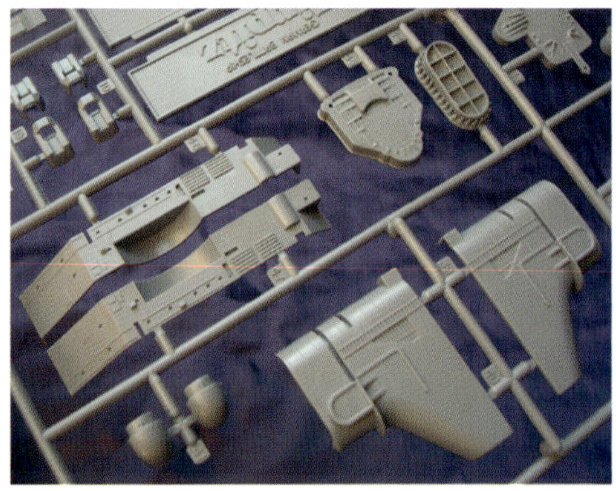

Photo-Etch & Resin Accessories

VOYAGER DETAIL SET FOR THE DML *BISMARCK*

1:700 Scale

The set for the Dragon DML *Bismarck* is Voyager Model PE 70001 DRA.

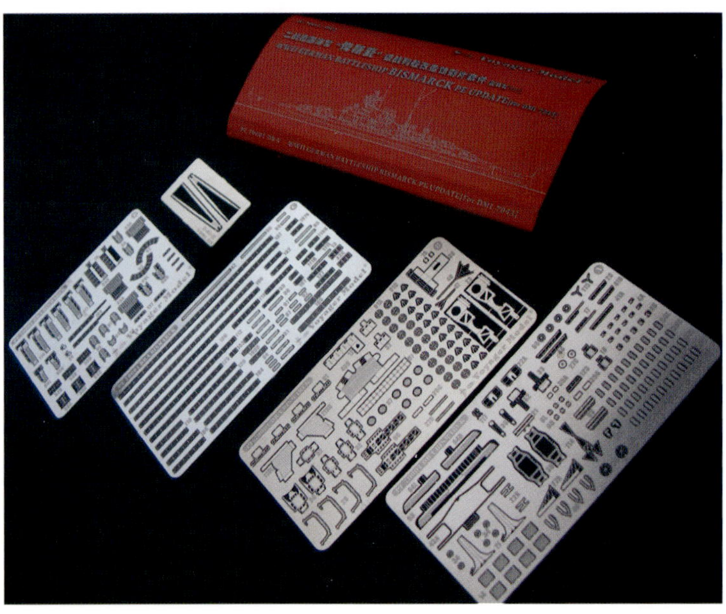

Instead of the usual flat envelope, the set comes in a thick orange packet containing five frets, plastic rod for cable reels, and two double-sided sheets of instructions. Each fret is identified by a letter, A to E, and the amazing number of parts are individually numbered. Relief etching is used throughout this set to add depth to some of the pieces. Highlights are as follows. Fret A includes relief-etched breakwaters, not only the main forward one but also side breakwaters. Fret B's relief-etched items include platforms for bridge and aft superstructure deck, with the joints between the wooden planks clearly incised; also the end pieces of the catapult and eight searchlight faces. Fret C comprises only superstructure railing and vertical ladder. Fret D concentrates on radar components and inclined ladders. Fret E is by far the smallest and just has the crane arms.

Sample: **Courtesy of Voyager Model**
www.voyagermodel.com

VOYAGER DETAIL SET FOR THE TRUMPETER *BISMARCK*

1:700 Scale

If you purchased the Pit-Road/Trumpeter *Bismarck*, Voyager Model has a different photo-etch super-detail set for that kit. This set, Voyager PE 70002 TRU-PR, comes in a blue packet and consists of six individual frets, A to F. There is some commonality of parts between the DML and Trumpeter sets, but there are many unique to one or other. Instructions make five pages total. Highlights by fret are:

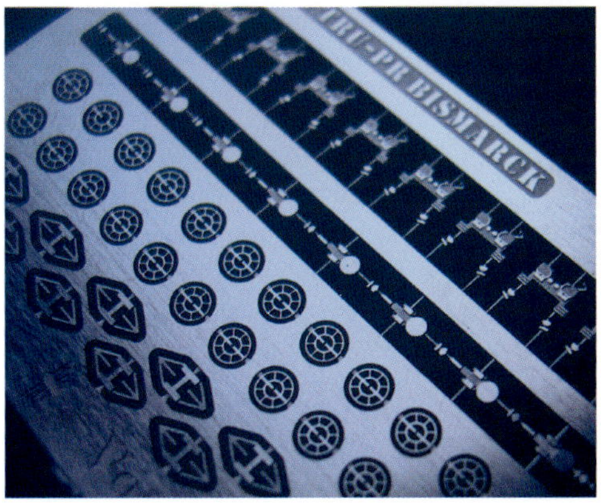

Fret A has the three different breakwaters with their individual brackets, catapult parts, mechanisms on crane cabs, searchlight faces and louvered vents. Fret B contains relief-etched parts for hangar end, aft platform deck with relief planking, and a multitude of ship's doors in different styles. Fret C includes absolutely spectacular relief-etched anti-skid decks for the amidships 4.1in gun positions. Fret D contains the superstructure railing cut to the exact lengths needed. Fret E contains mechanisms and individual gunners' seats for 37mm AA guns and twelve four-piece cable reels. Fret F is the smallest as it contains only the crane arms plus pulleys.

Sample: **Courtesy of Voyager Model** www.voyagermodel.com

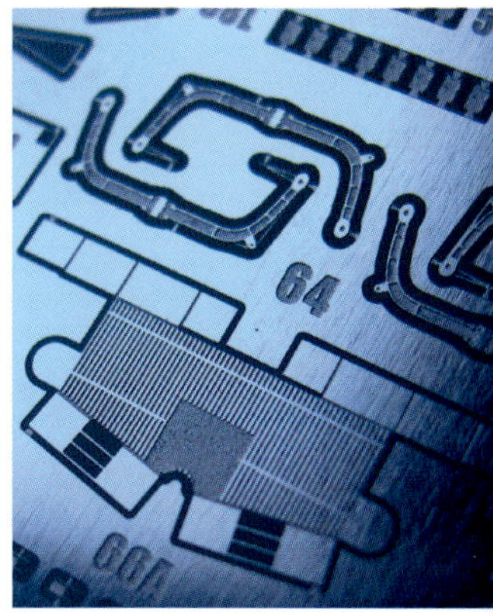

LION ROAR DETAIL SET FOR THE SINGLE 20MM C30 AA GUNS

1:700 Scale

This stainless steel photo-etch set in 1:700 scale (LE-700012) provides 52 of the C30 20mm German light AA guns, which can also be used for the similar looking C38 guns. Lion Roar has designed the guns so that extra width is provided to the breech-block and pedestal by providing an extra layer for the thicker parts of the gun. The base plates are also part of each one-piece gun and fold outwards from the base of the pedestal. Lion Roar also throws in an assortment of other DKM fittings on this fret.

Sample: **Courtesy of Lion Roar** www.lionroar.net

LION ROAR DETAIL SET FOR THE QUADRUPLE 20MM VIERLING

1:700 Scale

The 2cm Flak 35 im Vierling L/38 had four C38 guns on a new mount, and was fitted on the *Tirpitz*. The Lion Roar set LE700013 for this weapon consists of two frets of relief-etched parts, the larger of five different parts in brass to assemble the chassis of the mount, and the smaller of stainless steel gun barrels and gunners' seats. This set makes up sixteen quad 20mm mounts, but only eleven can have gun shields on the front, as not all quad mounts were equipped with the front shield. The gun chassis goes together in a series of layers so the finished mount will be three-dimensional. On the stainless steel fret there are 25 sets of barrels and 48 gunner's seats, so you'll have a substantial supply of spares in these areas. The guns fit on the outside of the gun mounting plates within

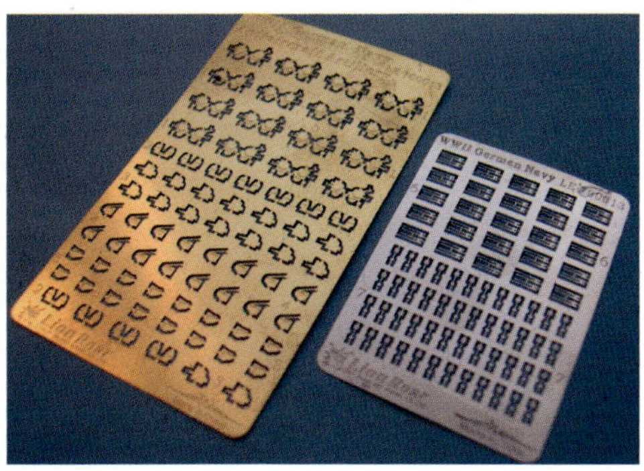

relief-etched recesses, so the final mount will actually be seven layers thick. Each gunner's seat consists of foot platform, seat and back rest, which are bent to shape.

Sample: **Courtesy of Lion Roar** www.lionroar.net

VOYAGER DETAIL SET FOR THE *TIRPITZ* 1:700 Scale

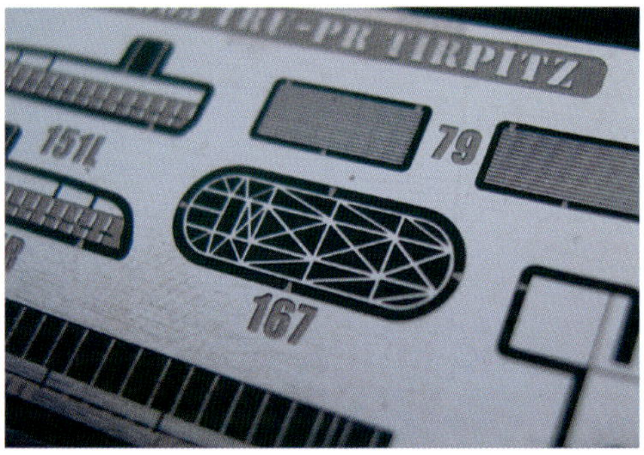

For the *Tirpitz* Voyager PE 70003 TRU-PR is a small supplemental fret, but you need to get the correct *Bismarck* set as well. I have not seen another set designated specifically DRA for the Dragon kit, so the parts will probably apply to both Trumpeter and Dragon. This set contains only two frets but these contain *Tirpitz*-specific parts, plus a small double-sided sheet of instructions.

Sample: **Courtesy of Voyager Model**
www.voyagermodel.com

LION ROAR DETAIL SET FOR THE CABLE/HOSE REELS 1:700 Scale

Although cable reels are found in some resin and brass 1:700 kits, they are very rarely represented in plastic kits as more than amorphous blobs. Lion Roar has a brass photo-etch set (LE-700008) of detailed cable and hose reels in 1:700 scale for any German warship kit, plastic or resin. The brass fret contains reels in three different sizes: sixteen large, eighteen medium, and thirty-six small. Although the medium and small reels appear to share the same basic design, the large reels are completely different. All seventy reels in the fret are relief-etched with the reel frame overlapping the reel ends.

Sample: **Courtesy of Lion Roar**
www.lionroar.net

WHITE ENSIGN MODELS *BISMARCK*/*TIRPITZ* PHOTO-ETCH SET 1:700 Scale

WEM PE 752 provides a complete set of fittings to doll up any self-respecting 1:700 scale *Bismarck* or *Tirpitz*. The fret provides a huge number of specialised parts for the Trumpeter/Sky Wave and Dragon kits and, although the Aoshima kits are not mentioned, this fine product would go well with that kit as well. One of the nicest pieces is the catapult with separate metal cover plates and aircraft cradles. WEM supplies all of the unique parts that differentiate the *Bismarck* from the *Tirpitz* – both folding navigation bridge wing designs, platforms unique to each ship, and four different radar arrays. Main, secondary and tertiary gun turrets and mounts all get at least four additional details per mount. There are even extra details for the main gun barbettes. The six-piece funnel grating is infinitely better than any of the plastic stack gratings. With cable reels, Marx floats, windlass drums, inclined ladders, vertical ladder, anchor chain, not to mention a host of various deck railings, this fret provides a full ensemble of detail for any of the new kits.

Sample: **Courtesy of White Ensign Models**
www.whiteensignmodels.com

L'ARSENAL ARADO AR-196 RESIN FLOATPLANES 1:350 Scale

In a new 1:350 accessory package, AC 350-27, L'Arsenal provides the resin and brass parts for two 1:350 scale Arado 196 floatplanes. Each of the Arados comes with three resin pieces, the aircraft plus two pontoons and five brass pieces, the propeller and four pontoon struts. Also available in 1:400 scale (AC 400-28) for the Heller and Kangnam kits.

Sample: **Courtesy of L'Arsenal**
http://www.larsenal.com/

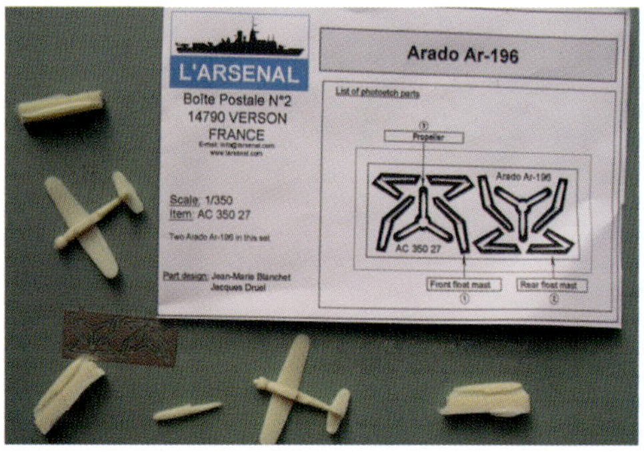

WHITE ENSIGN MODELS *BISMARCK* ULTIMATE SET

1:350 Scale

White Ensign Models 1:350 scale *Bismarck* brass photo-etch set WEM 3529 sets a new standard in magnificent detail. Two large frets per set are crammed with detailed relief-etched parts. The larger, measuring 11in by 7in, contains all of the more delicate fittings, in fine-gauge brass. Almost all of the parts are applicable to both ships of the class but there are some parts that are for *Tirpitz* alone. Some of the most impressive parts are the large louvered vents, which are open between their individual slats and the slats themselves can be turned. Since there are twenty-two of these on the ship, these parts alone will make a tremendous difference on Tamiya kits. There is an extensive selection of radars on this fret, and also a wide variety of platforms and associated gear found in Frets A and B, which will add great variety to the model. There are a huge quantity of relief-etched doors, hatches and portholes of every description and purpose. Normally these are rather humble items but WEM makes them stunning. There are innumerable individual portholes, each of which has an 'eyebrow' (rigol) and open hinged deadlights in different styles.

The second fret measures 10⅞in by 4⅞in and is made from thicker gauge brass, because it contains the heavier superstructure features and fittings. The stars of this fret are items for the hangars and catapult. The hangar ends with relief-etched frames and panelling and open doors are fantastic, while the catapult is a large, prominent – and most importantly – beautifully done assembly of multiple brass parts. This fret also contains the aircraft handling cranes (each ship has its own style of crane), plus funnel gratings, as well as some of the heavier platforms and platform supports.

Sample: **Courtesy of White Ensign Models**
www.whiteensignmodels.com

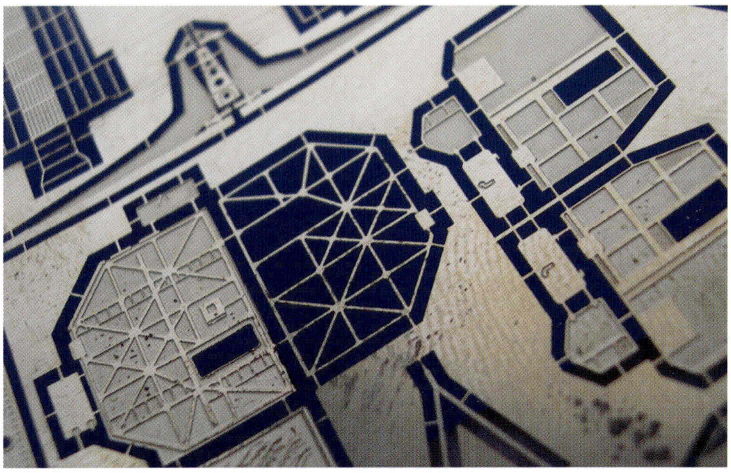

VOYAGER RAILINGS DETAIL SET FOR THE *BISMARCK/TIRPITZ*

1:700 Scale

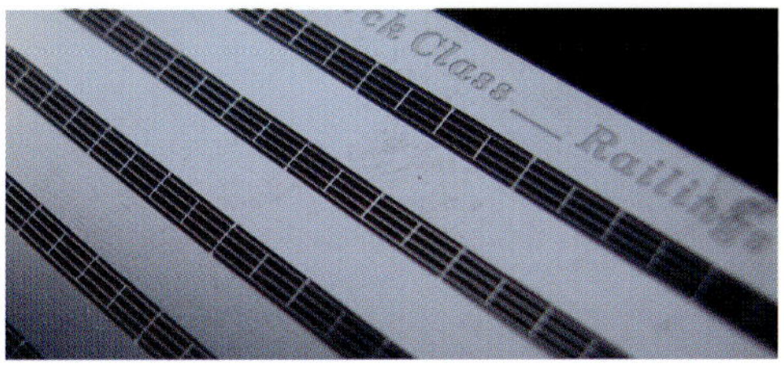

The above sets contain all of the superstructure railing, but Voyager also produce a set (AP020) for the long runs of railing on the main deck that can be used for either manufacturer's kit.

Sample: **Courtesy of Voyager Model**
www.voyagermodel.com

WHITE ENSIGN MODELS *BISMARCK/TIRPITZ* SUPERSTRUCTURE DECK PLATING

1:350 Scale

WEM PE 3565 provides an additional fret of brass photo-etch decks for the superstructure of the Tamiya *Bismarck* and *Tirpitz* kits. Typically for WEM, what they claim as a supplemental product instantly becomes essential once you see it, as it is on a different plane from most detail sets. This provides the textured decks for all levels of the German battleships' superstructure that is void of detail on Tamiya kits. The large surface area of the textured brass decks, produced to the highest standards, make a tremendous visual impact.

Many of the deck pieces replicate the wood planking, but there is also more ornate and complex steel grating or wooden duck boards. The change in texture and appearance in each of these decks, often in prominent positions, does create a very dramatic appearance. The *Tirpitz* had more AA positions than *Bismarck* and these positions had their own unique style of steel treadways, those on the forward superstructure roof including special angled splinter shielding since the position is on a slope. Other solid steel items found on the fret are a number of replacement splinter shields for plastic ones that must be removed to install the new decks. Additionally WEM provides several special splinter shields with solid lower half and two-bar railing above.

Sample: **Courtesy of White Ensign Models**
www.whiteensignmodels.com

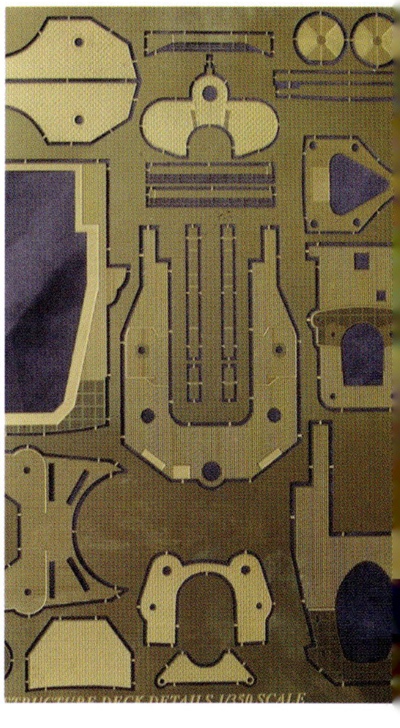

WHITE ENSIGN MODELS DKM DOORS AND WINDOWS

1:400 Scale

The 1:400 scale photo-etch brass fret of Kriegsmarine portholes and doors provides a tremendous variety of these overlooked fitting, every one magnificently relief-etched. The fret contains: 28 doors with open portholes; 2 small doors/ hatches; 76 rectangular windows and 127 round portholes, each in three different styles that can be modelled open or closed. It will take time to attach these portholes, one at a time, over the featureless holes on the Heller and Kangnam kits but they will but they will pump up the detail of both the kits dramatically.

Sample: **Courtesy of White Ensign Models** www.whiteensignmodels.com

LION ROAR BRASS BARRELS & TURRET DETAIL

1:700 Scale

Lion Roar produces a set of brass barrels that will definitely enhance your *Bismarck* and *Tirpitz*. Included in Lion Roar set LE700021 are eight brass 15in barrels, with muzzles already bored-out, and a 28-piece brass fret of turret details. Twenty are sliding observation shutters for range finders and open and closed shutters for the front faces of the turrets. The other eight parts are inclined ladders for the turret sides.

Sample: **Courtesy of Lion Roar** www.lionroar.net

WHITE ENSIGN MODELS DKM ANTI-AIRCRAFT WEAPONS

1:700 Scale

WEM PE 733 provides relief-etched brass parts for four different DKM AA mounts. Provided are multiple parts for eight C/30 quadruple 20mm mounts, eight C/38 quadruple 20mm mounts, eight M/43 twin 37mm mounts and twenty-two single 20mm guns.

Sample: **Courtesy of White Ensign Models** www.whiteensignmodels.com

WHITE ENSIGN MODELS DKM DOORS AND WINDOWS

1:700 Scale

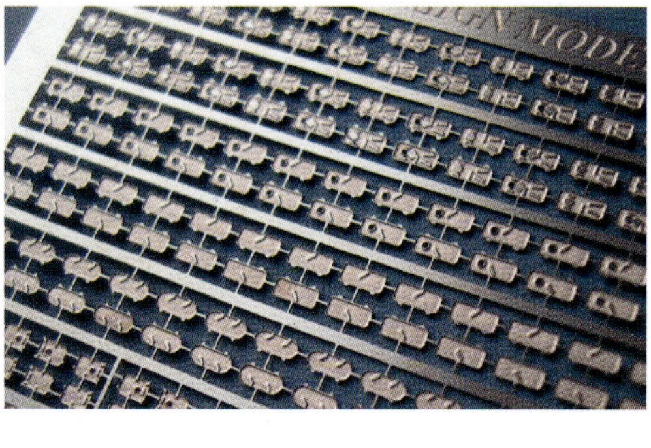

This set is not a smaller version of the WEM set in 1:400 scale. All doors and windows are in closed position with WEM PE 764 and concentrates on doors. There are 140 doors in five different patterns and 34 square windows. All of these small brass parts are beautifully executed with fine relief-etching.

Sample: **Courtesy of White Ensign Models** www.whiteensignmodels.com

Modelmakers' Showcase

SAMEK *BISMARCK* 1:700 Scale

By PATRICIO CARLUCCI

Often driving from Germany to Denmark for business reasons, I was always tempted by the Kiel canal, especially in winter, as a stage for a diorama. Having built the *Gorizia* and gained some confidence with resin, I decided on an epic subject: the *Bismarck* in the cold March of 1941 on her final trip to Kiel through the canal, before getting her final camouflage. This deserved maximum respect and accuracy. Considering myself a rookie in the hobby, I really feel grateful for the quantity of information shared by the many people who have dedicated a good part of their lives to researching every possible aspect of the subject.

The Diorama: The base is a picture frame, the glass being the base of the oil painting representing the water. Multiple layers of Future were used for glossiness. There is a layer of creased aluminum foil behind the

glass that is hard to notice on the pictures but in real life renders a good 3D effect behind the transparent oil paint layer. The banks are formed from normal white plaster, while the vegetation is the only type I have found that works at 1/700 after a long quest in the incredible quantity of railway modelling stores in Germany. The docks are in resin from H-P Models (Germany).

The Model: Samek's *Bismarck* is an excellent model, but even after paint, weathering and dry brushing it seemed tremendously bare to my eyes compared with the photos. It took me three days to get a finished, painted model and another two months of a couple of hours a day for the rest of the details. Here is a list of the material used:

- GMM: WW2 German warships – watertight doors – extra ladders – figures – cable reels – anchors – flag decals.
- Tom's Modelworks: *Bismarck-Tirpitz* set – rail netting – figures.
- H-P Models: *Seebaer* tug – German Navy Hafenlagen.
- Samek: *R 3-7* minesweepers-patrol boats (two per kit).
- MMN (Italy): White metal beautiful 1/700 miniatures of Tiger I, Pzw. IV and Famo.
- Sky Wave: European building.
- Pit-Road: Equipment for IJN vessels (!) (mainly paravanes and fire hoses)

The *Bismarck* overall grey is RAL 7001 (155) Vallejo acrylic. The decks are painted with Model Master 'Deck Tan' heavily modified with varying shades of brown and yellow for different areas. To weather the decks I used several oil washes in different tones of brown, chestnut ink from Citadel and black china ink diluted in Isopropyl alcohol. Every time a layer of weathering dried, I used the finest grain sandpaper available to smooth the wood to a satin finish and enhance the contrasting grooves. Finally, with a 0.05 Copic liner I have traced the missing plank ends in one of the hardest passages of the build-up. The armour belt received the same liner treatment to simulate plating since it really looked too flat once the deck was so nicely detailed. Masts are completely scratch-built from copper and stretched sprue.

TAMIYA *BISMARCK* 1:350 scale

By ED KEEGAN

There were a number of things I did beyond what Tamiya supplies you with in the box. I used HO scale ties for the deck, the three White Ensign Models photo-etch sets and one Gold Medal Models photo-etch set to enhance the model. My research was mainly based on Internet references, and help from several fellow modellers for accuracy. I know I should have spent some money on publications, but I don't feel I've graduated to that level of detail yet. The hardest part, in terms of time, was the decking, which took about six months. Warren Jones's work on his *New Jersey* inspired me to try real wood, and Kann Gok's *Bismarck* further inspired me to use lengths of lumber, rather than full strips, though I cheated and used 20mm lengths instead of the 10mm lengths Kann used. I like the effect so much I will continue to use it when I can on future projects, but the 'shift of butts' pattern should be more uniform across the deck rather than angled.

I attempted to scratch build some items around the conning tower and some other areas but I didn't do as good a job as I would have liked on them. Rigging was accomplished using nylon sewing thread run through a permanent ink marker. Definition of how the *Bismarck* was rigged was probably where a publication would have been more helpful than what I was using. I replaced the main gun barrels with

brass rod, but I made a mistake and used three widths rather than two – but they are very nice items and would add a lot to the overall look of any model. I used play dough to create the blast bags. This is the first time I have created blast bags and I was pretty pleased with how the material worked. It required a little attention when trying to form it around the barrel, but sealed with CA and painted they look pretty good. I used chain from Model Expo to replace the moulded-on anchor chains. The searchlights were drilled and painted with Testors Silver and then filled with Future.

Paint was Tamiya, with a custom mix for the hull but otherwise as suggested in the kit, except I used Sky Grey for the superstructure. The swastikas and circles on the deck were masked and painted. I used markings and flags from Begemot's Kriegsmarine Flags and Markings sold by WEM for the ship and the planes. This scheme should represent the *Bismarck* as she might have been after March of 1941. Overall it took about ten months to complete, although I was slowed at the end when a steam launch popped off the model as I was adding the rails and was never heard from again. Fortunately Tamiya sells sprues of its kits and one arrived about a week after the launch went missing. I'll probably find the original piece sometime soon!

TRUMPETER *BISMARCK* 1:700 scale By BYOUNG DAE LEE

For added detail Byoung Dae Lee used Voyager Model *Bismarck* photo-etch set and White Ensign Models DKM anti-aircraft gun photo-etch set for replacing the kit's AA gun parts. He added some minor modifications around the armaments with plastic rod. The kit represents her final appearance. Notice how the light grey overpainting received in Norway has started to wear off from the pounding in the Atlantic.

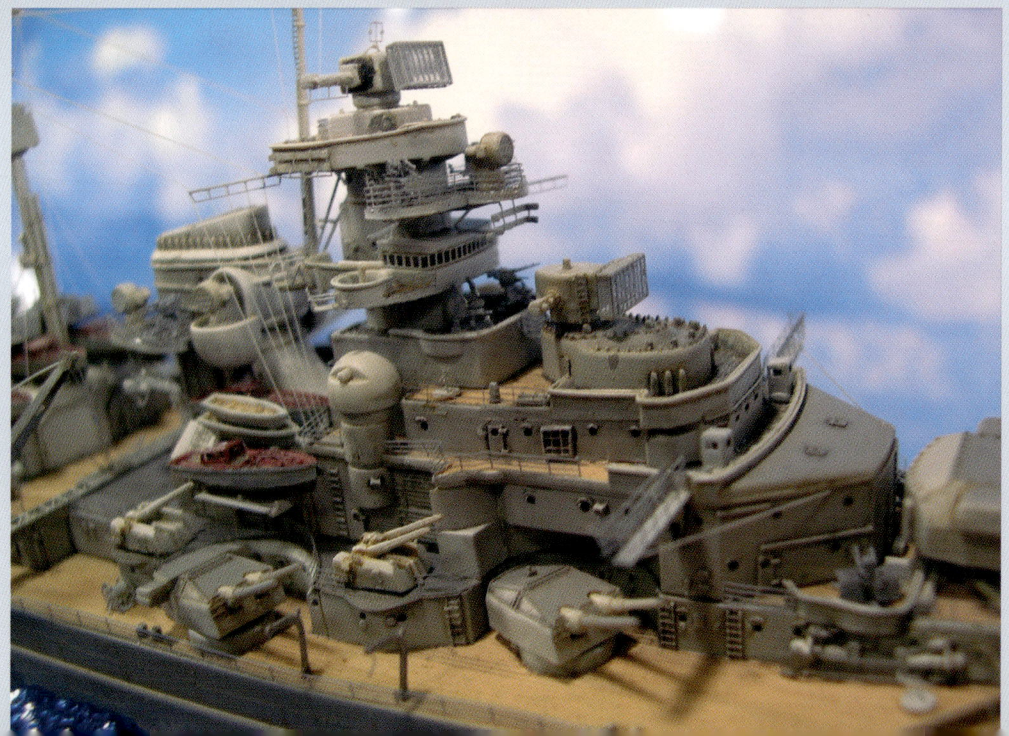

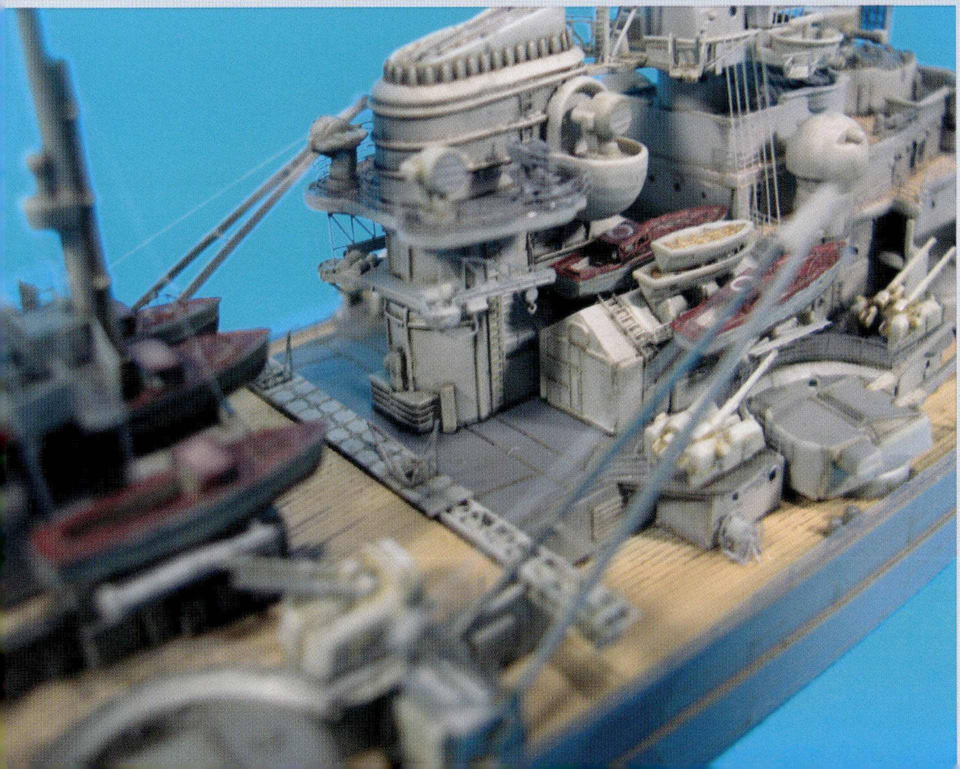

TAMIYA *TIRPITZ* 1:350 scale

By LOUIS CARABOTT

From the Island of the Knights of Saint John comes the *Tirpitz* in the Lair, showing her under attack in the Norwegian fjord with anti-torpedo nets deployed. Louis Carabott, who is a very active member of IPMS Malta, built the 1:350 scale Tamiya *Tirpitz*. Ray Farrugia built the 1:48 scale Swordfish used in the combination shot. Photographs are by David Grech. Work of these and other members of IPMS Malta can be seen at their web site at www.ipmsmalta.com.

TRUMPETER *BISMARCK* 1:700 scale

By NORBERT THIEL

Norbert Thiel runs one of the largest internet shops in naval modelling – NNT in Bad Sackingen, Germany – which features a huge selection of naval kits and accessories, as well as producing his own line of resin ship models and accessories (www.nntmodell.com). However, Norbert is also an avid modeller himself. This is the Trumpeter *Bismarck* which he built, with many Gold Medal Models photo-etch parts, Samek cranes, NNT gun barrels, Eduard figures, an Aoshima tug with some scratch-building and a lot of fun. Photographs are by Martin Kohring.

TAMIYA *BISMARCK* 1:350 scale

By MIKE GOLDEN

I started my build with the references from the books *Battleship Bismarck* by Ulrich Elfrath & Bodo Herzog and *Warship Pictorial: Kriegsmarine Bismarck* by Steve Wiper. The kit I used was the 1/350 scale model by Tamiya armed with the photo-etch sets from Gold Medal Models and White Ensign Models. Brass barrels were from the late Steve Nutall, whom I will miss. Along with painting in Colourcoat paints, the build took five and a half months from start to finish and I enjoyed every minute of it.

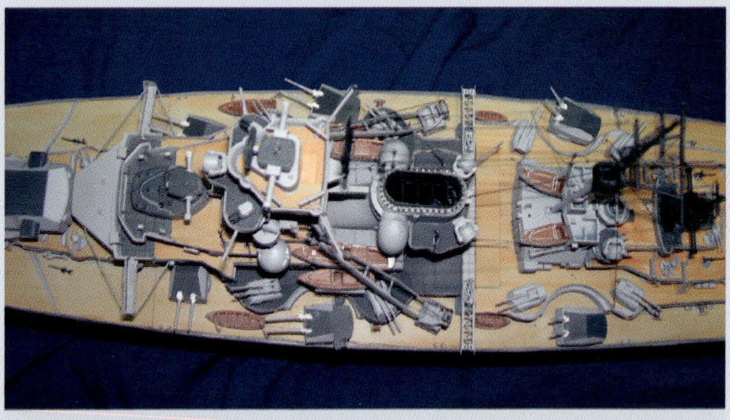

TRUMPETER *BISMARCK* 1:700 scale

By FRANTIŠEK KUT

This is the Trumpeter 1:700 scale *Bismarck* built by František Kut of the Czech Republic and shows the ship's appearance in her transit to Norway. The model is primarily built right from the box with no after-market photo-etch. The model reflects how, with a nice paint job, the newest *Bismarck* kits build into fine replicas without additional detail.

Drawn by Miroslaw Skwiot
Artwork by Zbigniew Kolacha

Bismarck March – May 1941
'Bar camouflage' carried by *Bismarck* between March and May 1941, in the final stages of the Baltic manoueuvres and the early stages of the Rheinübung operation.

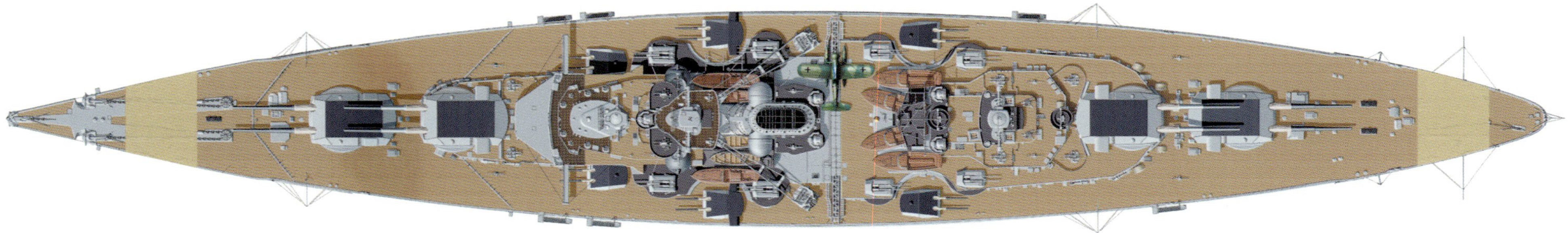

Bismarck April – May 1941
The battleship *Bismarck* camouflage painting with red 'A' main battery turret that she probably wore in April and May 1941, during Rheinübung operation preparations.

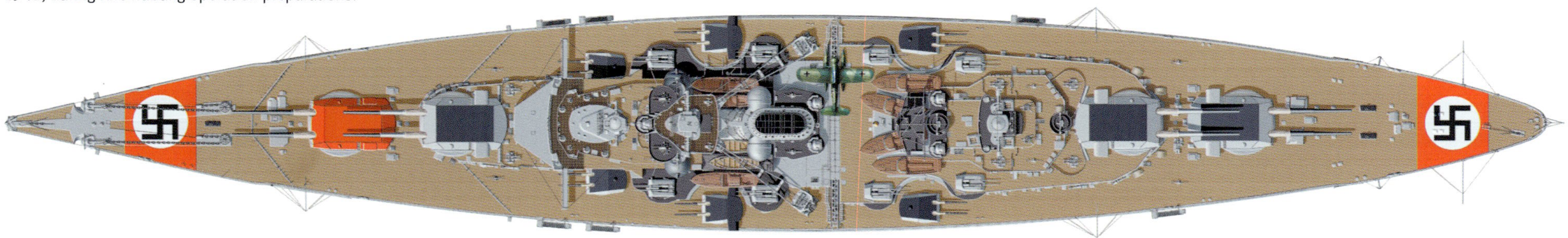

Drawn by Miroslaw Skwiot
Artwork by Zbigniew Kolacha

Bismarck May 1941
The *Bismarck* as painted as she arrived in Grimstadfjord on 21 May 1941.

Bismarck May 1941
The *Bismarck* painted as she approached the French coast between 26 May 1941 and her sinking. Earlier camouflage is showing through the later light grey paint.

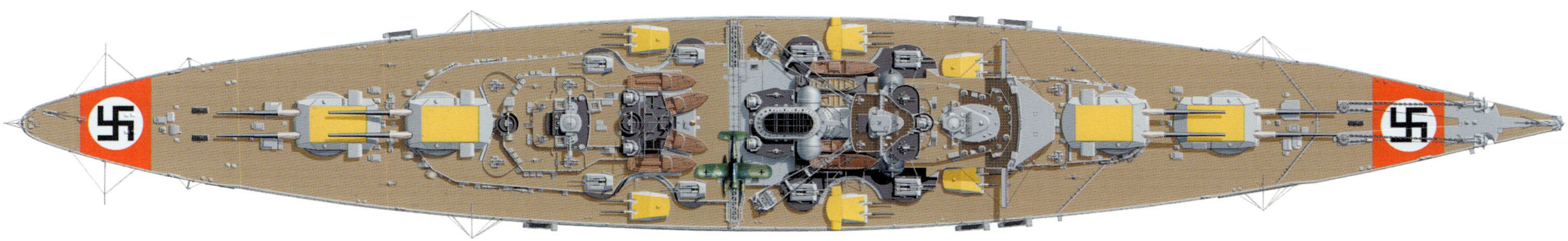

Drawn by Miroslaw Skwiot
Artwork by Zbigniew Kolacha

Tirpitz May – June 1942

Camouflage painting as applied to the *Tirpitz* in the springtime (late May – early June 1942), after the deployment to Faettenfjord, Norway. Irregular spots were painted, so as to blend her with the spring vegetation on the hill in the background.

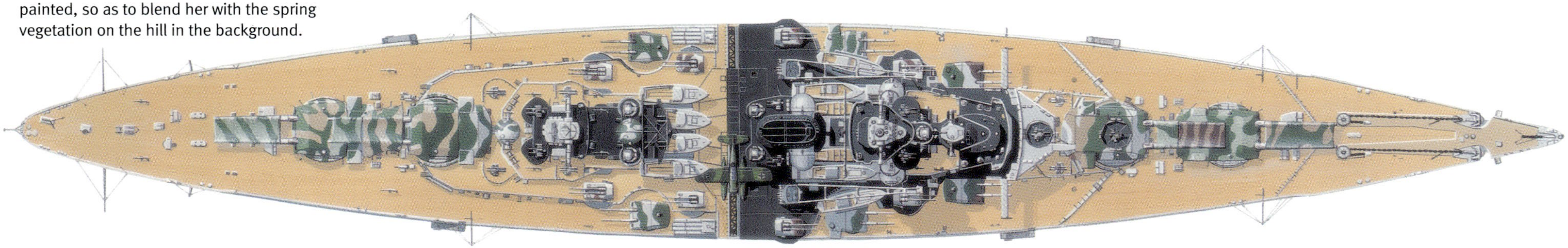

Tirpitz June 1942

Camouflage scheme applied to the *Tirpitz* in late June 1942, while in Faettenfjord. The scheme blended well with the surrounding hills. It is interesting to note that the camouflage schemes were strictly localised – each redeployment, as well as the changing seasons, required the repainting of the whole ship.

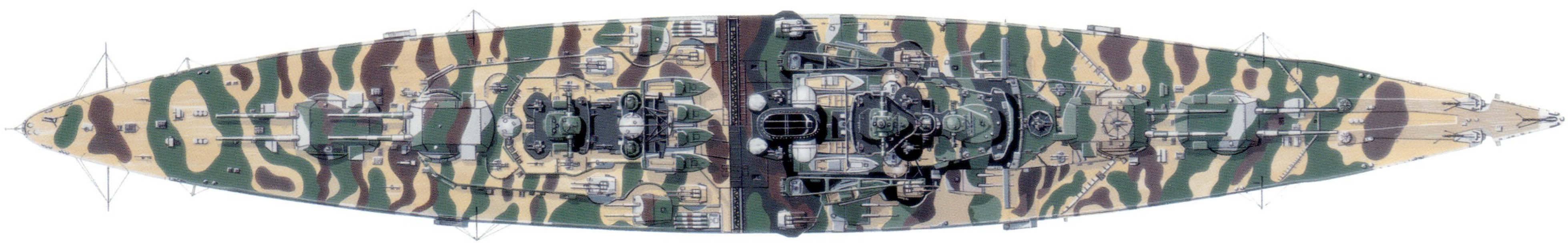

Tirpitz July 1942

The wedge camouflage applied to the *Tirpitz* in mid-July 1942, after redeployment in Norway, from Faettenfjord to Bogenfjord, near Narvik. This move to a colder region required a revised scheme to suit the features of the surrounding backdrop. Minor alterations to the paint details on the 15in gun turrets help to identify precise mooring places in photographs taken during this period.

Drawn by Miroslaw Skwiot
Artwork by Zbigniew Kolacha

Note: The green in the wedge camouflage schemes is a subject of debate, some believing the colour to be dark grey. See http://www.bismarck-class.dk/tirpitz/paint_schemes/paint_tirpitz_1943.html

Tirpitz Winter 1942

The wedge camouflage applied to the *Tirpitz* in winter 1942, after redeployment to Altafjord.

Tirpitz September 1943

The *Tirpitz* camouflage during the Spitzbergen foray (September 1943, Operation Sizilien/Zitronella). Turret roofs and sloping armour partly painted dark grey.

Drawn by Miroslaw Skwiot
Artwork by Zbigniew Kolacha

Tirpitz October 1943 - March 1944
Starboard side of the *Tirpitz* in the wedge camouflage scheme applied to her during the repair in Altafjord between October 1943 and March 1944. It was modified slightly after the Operation Tungsten raid in April.

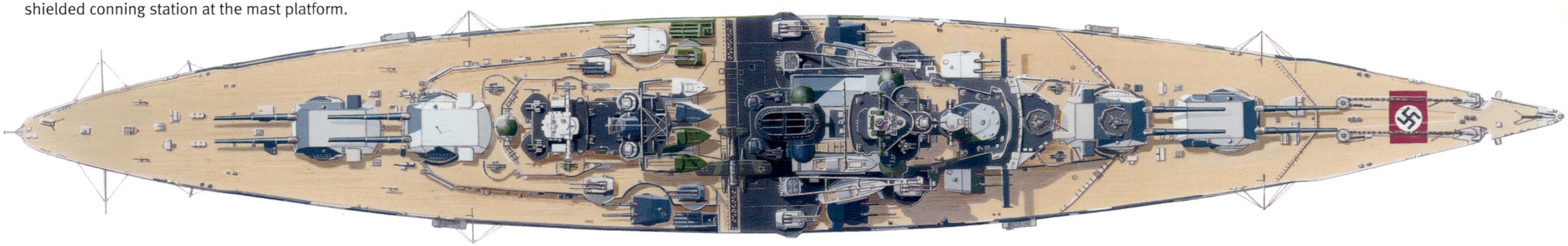

Tirpitz October 1943 - March 1944
Scheme as worn until April 1944. Note the plexiglass shielded conning station at the mast platform.

Tirpitz October 1943 – March 1944
Port side view of the *Tirpitz* in a camouflage scheme applied to her during the repair in Altafjord between October 1943 and March 1944.

Differences and Appearance Changes

The two ships of the class could easily be distinguished one from the other. There were anti-aircraft mounts mounted on Bruno turret and the forward bridge of *Tirpitz* on her deployment to Norway, but, even more noticeably, the *Tirpitz* had an extended shelter deck at the area of the catapult. Compared to other classes of battleships, however, there were very few changes made to them during their careers. The short life of the *Bismarck* precluded much modification, but *Tirpitz* followed the pattern of other navies during World War Two – increased light 20mm AA mounts and new radar arrays as it was fielded. Camouflage was the one area where *Bismarck* had many changes, going through many different variations of hull and superstructure painting, and turret crown colours in a period of just two months. The *Tirpitz* was a even more of a peacock among battleships, moving from drab Baltic schemes to a sequence of multi-colour camouflage sported in Norway.

During the harsh winter early in 1941, *Bismarck* spent a lot of time in harbour as the weather curtailed training. Notice that the swastika aerial recognition markings are already painted on the forecastle. Details of the top of the armoured conning tower can be seen in the foreground.

Bow Design and Anchor Arrangement: The *Bismarck* class battleships were designed with the same stem profile as the *Scharnhorst* class battleships, with very little rake. The early trials of *Scharnhorst* and *Gneisenau* showed that this shape was very poor at keeping green water off the forecastle, and both were refitted with the so-called Atlantik bow, which had a dramatic curved rake that gave the ships a much more graceful appearance. *Bismarck* was launched with a straight stem but was given the Atlantik bow during completion, while *Tirpitz* acquired the Atlantik bow while building. The new bow design necessitated a new anchor arrangement. The conventional hull side anchor hawse was replaced by channels at the bow with the anchors pulled on deck by the capstans. The flukes overhung the channel for balance and the anchor was given power assistance to lower the anchor through the channels. Additionally a fairing was constructed outboard at the lower entrance of each channel, probably to prevent the flukes from damaging the sides of the hull.

Shelter Deck: On the *Bismarck* the edge of the shelter deck in the area of the catapult stopped short of the hull sides. This is not so for *Tirpitz*, where the shelter deck, running from just aft of the second 5.9in

SUMMARY OF *BISMARCK* MODIFICATIONS

Date	AA Modification	Other modification
		Added Atlantik bow during fitting out
October-November 1940	Added two aft twin 105mm gun mounts missing at completion at Gotenhafen	Fitted foretop and conning tower rangefinders
March 1941	Added Army pattern single 20mm gun to top of Anton turret	
April 1941	Two Army pattern single 20mm guns added to aft superstructure	
May 1941	Two quadruple 20mm mounts added to searchlight platforms on upper tower and three Army pattern 20mm singles landed	

turret on each side to just aft of the catapult, was extended out to the edge of the hull. With the *Bismarck* the second 4.1in AA mount on the shelter deck was partially masked by the large aircraft/boat cranes that were mounted outboard on the weather deck to the rear of the AA mount. The extension of the shelter deck on *Tirpitz* allowed the second 4.1in to be mounted further outboard. The large cranes were moved from the weather deck to the shelter deck and inboard of the AA mount, so these 4.1in guns were no longer masked.

Heavy AA Mounts: Like other navies the Kriegsmarine did not have enough of the most modern ordnance and temporary substitutes had to be provided. The 4.1in/65 (105mm) SK C33 heavy anti-aircraft gun was a 1933 design, but it needed a new mount developed for it. Initially a 1931 twin mount developed for twin 88mm AA guns was adapted for the new ordnance. This mount was the 8.8cm Dopp.L. C/31. As the *Bismarck* was fitting out, the forward four 105mm mounts were installed first. These were of the modified 88mm variety with the imposing nomenclature of 10.5cm SK C/33 auf 8.8cm Dopp.L. C/31. *Tirpitz* also had two of these makeshift mounts installed as the after-most 105mm on each side.

The new mounting developed for the twin 105mm guns was the Dopp.L. C/37 so the complete nomenclature would be 10.5cm SK C/33 auf Dopp.L. C/37. The aft four 105mm positions on *Bismarck* were equipped with the new mounts at Gotenhafen during trials and *Tirpitz* received the new mounts for the

Above: This photograph of *Bismarck* shows the passageway below the catapult and the aircraft/boat crane mounted on the weather deck. With *Tirpitz* the shelter deck was extended to the hull side and the crane was relocated further inboard and one level higher on the shelter deck itself.

Right: The new model 4.1in gun mount, designated 10.5cm SK C/33 auf Dopp.L. C/37, is seen in profile. This mount designed specifically for the new ordnance was used for the aft four mounts in *Bismarck*. This mount can easily be distinguished from the modified 88mm mounts, 10.5cm SK C/33 auf 8.8cm Dopp.L. C/31, in that there is shielding over the breech mechanisms.

forward six positions. For the *Tirpitz* the aft two modified 88mm C/31 mounts were subsequently replaced by Dopp.L. C/37 mounts, but the *Bismarck* kept the forward older modified C/31 mounts.

Although the mounts were superficially similar, they can easily be distinguished one from another. The 8.8cm Dopp.L. C/31 is smaller and shorter, with raised conical fittings on each forward edge, and has open breech blocks. The much heftier Dopp.L. C/37 is larger and higher with sliding vision ports replacing the conical positions, and instead of angling backwards at a constant angle the sides of the newer mount veer upwards sharply two-thirds back from the front of the mount. Most noticeably, splinter shielding is provided over the breech blocks on the newer mounts. Of the new injected plastic 1:700 scale kits, the new Aoshima release has the right mix of C/31 and C/37 mounts for *Bismarck* but I have not been able to see if the Aoshima *Tirpitz* has the additional C/37 mounts. Dragon is right on the money with the correct mix for *Bismarck* and additional C/37 mounts for *Tirpitz*. On the other hand, both the Trumpeter and Sky Wave kits provide four C/31 and four C/37 mounts in both the *Bismarck* and *Tirpitz* kits. This is correct for *Bismarck* but this combination was never mounted by *Tirpitz*, and you'll be short two C/37 mounts in her Baltic appearance and four C/37 mounts for her Norway deployment.

Torpedo Tubes: *Bismarck* never carried torpedo tubes but two four-tube mounts were added to *Tirpitz* after commissioning

In the foreground is one of the 10.5cm SK C/33 auf 8.8cm Dopp.L. C/31 of *Bismarck*. This was a modified twin 88mm mount used as a stop-gap measure before a purpose built mount was developed. The *Bismarck* retained this pattern for the forward four mounts throughout her short career. The uncovered breech for the guns is a give away for this pattern.

The quarterdeck of *Tirpitz* is seen from the mainmast. In the foreground is the armoured aft fire control station. Between this position and Caesar turret is a HA AA director still in an open position. This was later given a spherical shield.

but before deployment to Norway. When Admiral Lütjens was the force commander of *Scharnhorst* and *Gneisenau* after a successful Atlantic breakout, he recommended that all heavy ships carry torpedoes. Twice armed merchant cruisers (AMC) had fought delaying actions, and the time needed to dispatch the AMC allowed the helpless merchantmen to scatter and few of these could be found after the AMC was finished. Torpedoes would have sunk these opponents far quicker. Accordingly, Hitler ordered that all heavy ships carry torpedo tubes for use against convoys.

In the summer of 1941 the *Tirpitz* received her quadruple 21in torpedo tubes at Kiel. One source stated these were recovered from German destroyer wrecks lost at Narvik in the spring of 1940 but this has not been verified. They were mounted on the weather deck just aft of the catapult, while just forward of the mounts, the extended shelter deck allowed for the stowage of spare torpedoes, with additional warheads in the magazines. Of course the torpedoes were never used and the presence of so much concentrated explosives in the form of the unprotected warheads, represented a far greater risk to *Tirpitz* than to convoys.

High Angle Directors: The *Bismarck* design featured four High Angle (HA) anti-aircraft gun directors: two on the forward superstructure (one on each side of the tower); and two on the centreline on the after superstructure. It was in the after HA directors that *Bismarck* differed from *Tirpitz*. The HA directors were designed to receive splinter shield cupolas to protect the crew and equipment from weather as well as enemy action. Only the two forward HA directors on *Bismarck* had cupolas, the after pair being in open tubs, and she was lost without them ever receiving the protective cupolas. *Tirpitz* had all four HA directors fitted with the cupolas. All of the

This presents a good view of Caesar turret and barbette. Note various deck fittings covered with canvas, including a single 20mm gun at right, as well as cable/hose reels. Ventilator trunking came up through the deck and was attached to the outside of the barbette.

SUMMARY OF *TIRPITZ* MODIFICATIONS

Date	AA Modification	Other modification
July-Aug 1941		Added torpedo tubes at Kiel
January 1942	Four quadruple 20mm mounts added, two on tower searchlight platform and two between aft director and Caesar turret and two additional 20mm single guns added on bridge	
February 1942	Added two quadruple 20mm mounts, one on Bruno turret and one on bridge at Norway; two single 20mm on bridge landed Added two quadruple 20mm mounts on funnel platform in place of single 20mm guns, which were landed Added two quadruple 20mm guns on quarterdeck	

Empty boat chocks on *Bismarck*'s weather deck abaft the 5.9in mount. On the superstructure one of the twin 4.1in mounts clearly displays the two conical structures on the front face that indicates the older model Dopp. L. C/31 mounting.

A wealth of detail can be seen on the forward superstructure sides and the base on Bruno barbette, including a paravane and the removeable panel in the breakwater. *Bismarck*'s solid support structure under the bridge navigation wing makes the ship identification easy.

new 1:700 scale kits have the correct configuration, although I have not verified this with the new Aoshima *Tirpitz*.

Light Anti-Aircraft: As with most navies, the Kriegsmarine developed three levels of anti-aircraft guns, heavy, medium and light. With few exceptions most navies never altered their heavy AA mounts during the war and this was true with the *Bismarck* class as the number of 4.1in (105mm) guns remained unchanged. For medium AA guns, the *Bismarck* class never increased the numbers of twin 37mm mounts either. It was only in the area of light AA that numbers increased, most often with the addition of quadruple 20mm mounts. When *Bismarck* was completed she carried twelve 20mm guns in single mounts, which compared favourably with the RN Vickers or the USN Browning machine guns, but this

Above: The medium AA gun of the class, the 37mm/L83 SK C30 gun. Behind this position is a canvas covered single 20mm gun.

Right: Right: The *Bismarck*'s funnel platforms. In *Tirpitz* the HA director and searchlight were on a single continuous platform.

Below: Below: Some of the ship's boats nested on top of the hangars flanking the funnel.

Below, right: The mainmast, The box-like observation station was removed from *Tirpitz* in December 1941.

Left: On each side of *Bismarck*'s funnel was a single hangar in which one Arado 196A could be stored. This photograph looks towards the bow and shows the end panel as well as boat stowage on the crown of the hangar.

Below: This is the FuMO-23 radar array with a 10-metre range-finder on the roof of the aft fire control station.

Bottom: The main aircraft hangar of *Bismarck*. The crown of this structure was used for stowage of the larger motor boats. Notice the walkway on the weather deck underneath the catapult, found on *Bismarck* but not *Tirpitz*.

was soon deemed too light. In March 1941 near the end of the Baltic trials, an additional Wehrmacht pattern single 20mm was added to the crown of Anton turret, and two additional single 20mm guns were added to the after superstructure in April 1941. All three of these army pattern single guns were landed in early May 1941, when she received two quadruple 20mm mounts on the searchlight platform near the top of the forward superstructure. This gave her a total of twenty 20mm guns at the time of her loss.

When the Germans conducted their after-action review of the *Bismarck* sortie, it was painfully evident that the ship had too few anti-aircraft guns. Therefore the decision was made to increase the light AA guns on *Tirpitz* from the original sixteen single 20mm guns. By early 1942, after her first increase, *Tirpitz* was carrying fourteen single 20mm guns and four quadruple 20mm mounts, for a total of thirty. Upon arrival in Norway a quadruple was added to the forward bridge and another quadruple mount replaced two single guns on the crown of Bruno turret, for a total of thirty-six 20mm guns. By 1944 the *Tirpitz* carried eighty 20mm guns with sixteen quadruple mounts and sixteen singles. Some of the singles may have been replaced by twin mounts shortly before her loss.

Radar Arrays: The radar fitted to the *Bismarck* and *Tirpitz* was effective, but did have a problem of height determination for HA targets, although early directional accuracy problems were ironed out by 1940. Secondary FuMo-25 and FuMo-26 radar was installed, which was primarily for search with limited fire control ability. Due to a narrow beam, lack of display units and plotter, the radar could not determine target course and speed, so range finding depended on the Zeiss optical rangefinders. The power output for the *Bismarck* primary

This sequence of photographs shows the preparation of an Arado 196A for launching on *Bismarck*.

Top left: With wings folded one of the aircraft is guided from the small hangar on the starboard side of the funnel.

Top right: This shows positioning of the Arado on the catapult and preparation for launch. Metal plates would normally cover the catapult when not in use but these have been removed for catapult operation.

Right: Detail of the *Bismarck*'s catapult with metal plates covering the centre section crossing the deck. Notice the walkway of the weather deck one deck lower found in *Bismarck* only.

Above: The Arado just leaving the launch trolley. Notice how the end of the catapult telescopes outwards, lengthening the catapult for launch.

radar was 14kW but the set on *Tirpitz* was increased to 100kW providing far greater signal strength. After the loss of *Bismarck*, the radar on *Tirpitz* did receive limited range finding ability and a supplemental parabolic Wurzberg radar was added for height determination for HA use. *Tirpitz* acquired an additional FuMO-27 mattress array around January 1942 and smaller Timor antennae. An enlarged FuMO-26 mattress was added in spring or summer 1944.

Camouflage Schemes: At various times both *Bismarck* and *Tirpitz* sported very colourful paint designs, although as completed both ships had an overall light grey paint scheme, albeit with slightly darker hull colour than the superstructure grey. Funnel caps were painted a dull aluminium. In early 1941 *Bismarck* received her dramatic black and white identification stripes on hull and superstructure with dark bow and stern to provide false length and a false bow wave on the light grey panel. Because of the very cold winter, the painting was done in stages. At this time her turret tops were dark grey, but in April 1941, near the end of her Baltic trials, she may have had her turret crowns painted carmine or wine-red for aircraft recognition. There is not total agreement on this but colour photographs of her companion *Prinz Eugen* clearly show the cruiser turret crowns in this colour. Another variation is that *Bismarck* may have been painted on only the crown of A turret. In preparation for her Atlantic sortie, the superstructure stripes were over-painted but the hull stripes were

SUMMARY OF *BISMARCK* CAMOUFLAGE PATTERNS

Date	Location	Pattern
August 1940	Baltic	Overall grey at commissioning and start of trials
Early 1941	Early Baltic Scheme	Bar camouflage with black and white stripes on hull and superstructure sides painted in stages due to extremely cold weather
April 1941	Later Baltic Scheme	Bar camouflage with black and white stripes on hull and superstructure sides; swastika aerial recognition panels on forecastle and quarterdeck; carmine or wine-red turret crowns (carmine crown may have been only on Anton)
Early May 1941	Later Baltic Scheme	Bar camouflage with black and white stripes on hull and superstructure sides; swastika aerial recognition panels on forecastle and quarterdeck
15 to 21 May 1941	Transit to Grimstadfjord	Baltic stripes still on hull sides but painted over on superstructure; swastika aerial recognition deck panels covered by tarpaulins
22 May 1941	Grimstadfjord, Norway	Hull stripes over-painted light grey in preparation for Atlantic sortie
26 May 1941	North Atlantic – preparations for entering Luftwaffe-controlled airspace	Pale yellow main and secondary turret crowns, aerial recognition swastikas on forecastle and quarterdeck; Baltic striping beginning to show through overall grey over-paint

SUMMARY OF *TIRPITZ* CAMOUFLAGE PATTERNS

Date	Location	Pattern
April 1939	Launch, Wilhelmshaven	Light grey overall
1940	Fitting out, Wilhelmshaven	Red brick building pattern on port side and splotches on starboard upper superstructure – the most bizarre camouflage scheme
Fall 1941	Trials in Baltic	Overall light grey with dark grey turret crowns
January 1942	Faettenfjord, Norway	Overall light grey; snow left on decks, canvas laid over main turrets, small evergreen trees 'planted' on quarterdeck and forecastle
March 1942	Faettenfjord, Norway – Operation Sportpalast	Overall light grey; false length with bow and stern hull sides over-painted dark grey
May – Early June 1942	Faettenfjord, Norway	Irregular green wave blotches added to turret crowns, turret sides and upper superstructure; false length with bow and stern hull sides over-painted dark grey
Late June 1942	Faettenfjord, Norway – Operation Rösselsprung	Entire superstructure over-painted dark grey or green with some brown panels; turret crowns dark green; small swastika recognition panel or large flag on port side quarterdeck; later in month all surfaces had wavy blotches in grey, green and brown – a very busy camouflage scheme
July 1942	Bogenfjord, Narvik, Norway	Bar camouflage – green and grey ray camouflage redone for colder environment
September 1943	Kaafjord, Norway – Operation Sizilien/Zitronella	Bar camouflage with hull ray camouflage in dark grey and superstructure rays in dark grey and dark green; turret crowns dark grey
October 1943 – March 1944	Altafjord, Norway	Bar camouflage – green and grey ray camouflage for hull and superstructure, swastika recognition panel on forecastle
April 1944	Altafjord, Norway	Splinter camouflage with dark grey rays on light grey
May-August 1944	Altafjord, Norway	Overall dark grey one level above shelter deck, including all of Anton and Dora turrets; barbettes for Bruno and Caesar turrets: light grey above this; green splotches added to decks in July 1944
November 1944	Altafjord, Norway	A variation of the May-August scheme but upper superstructure repainted different, unidentified, colour

This photograph looks up to the rear face of the 10-metre main rangefinder position. A FuMO-23 radar was mounted on the front face.

Bismarck: The drawing directly below shows the forward face of the funnel flanked on either side with HA AA directors protected by the segmented splinter shield cupolas. The middle drawing shows the rear face of the superstructure tower capped by another 10-metre main gun rangefinder. *(Drawings by Miroslaw Skwiot)*

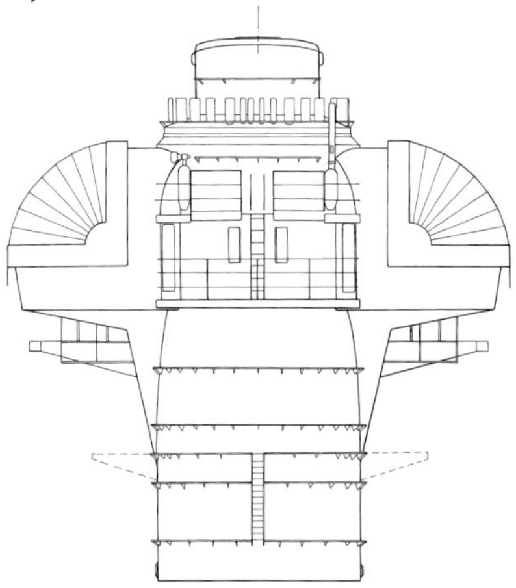

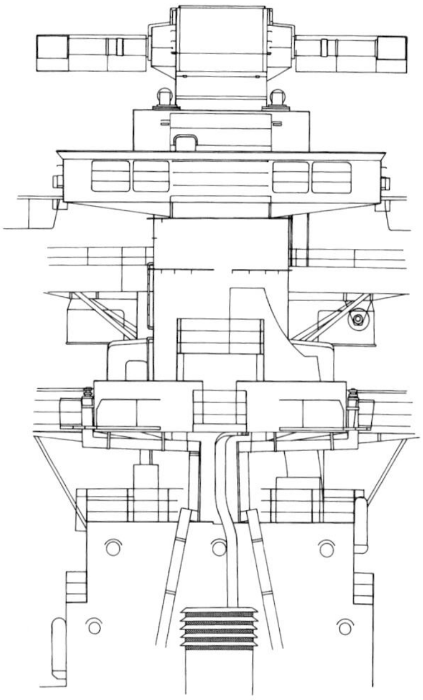

retained; crowns were repainted dark grey. Upon arrival at Norway the hull stripes on *Bismarck* were over-painted, so she sortied in overall grey. There was one last change: when it appeared that *Bismarck* had broken free of the Royal Navy hunt and would shortly be within the range of Luftwaffe fighter protection, the main turret crowns were again repainted for aerial recognition purposes, but this time with a golden yellow paint. Some have expressed doubts about the yellow crowns but, on the whole, eye-witness evidence favours it and it is entirely in line with previous and subsequent Kriegsmarine painting practices.

Tirpitz was a true peacock and had one of the most unusual paint schemes in the war. As she was fitting out she increasingly became the target of air raids. In an effort to camouflage her, the port side of *Tirpitz*, which faced the basin, was painted to mimic the red brick buildings behind her. Since her starboard side was moored at the quay, that side of the hull did not receive this bizarre paint scheme but the starboard superstructure did receive an irregular splotch pattern. In her Baltic trials she did not have the Baltic black and white paint scheme but did have dark grey turret crowns. When she deployed to Norway, *Tirpitz* received the first camouflage paint scheme of many designed to blend her into her surroundings. The camouflage pattern would change with the season and location: stark greys in winter with snow allowed to accumulate on the decks; with the advent of spring, greens and brown would appear in the colour spectrum. *Tirpitz* even had evergreens decorating the forecastle and quarterdeck after her arrival. With her deployment farther north to Narvik in July 1942 the bar or ray camouflage made its appearance. *Tirpitz* would carry variations of the bar scheme, changing colours with the season, until May 1944 when her hull was repainted a very dark grey up to the 02 deck, including Anton and Dora turrets and the barbettes for Bruno and Caesar turrets. The greys used for the Baltic paint schemes were slightly different in hue from the ones used for *Tirpitz* in Norway. For the fastidious or exacting modeller, White Ensign Models produces a line of paints in their Colourcoat line for warships of the Kriegsmarine, which includes the various Baltic and Norwegian greys.

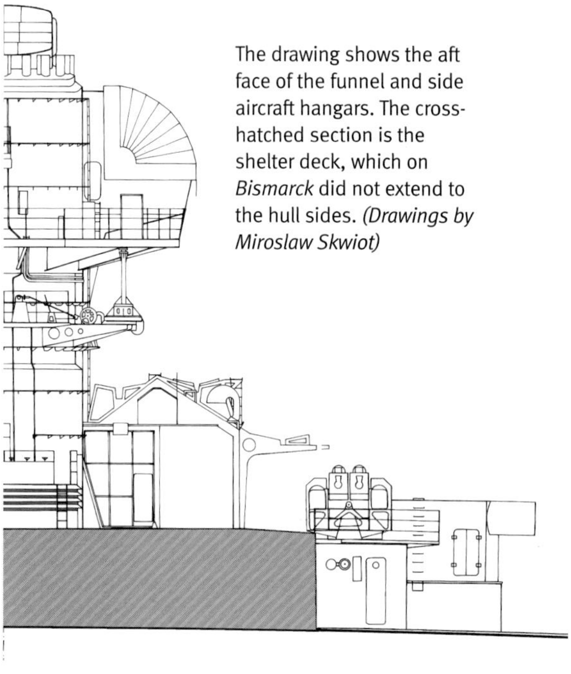

The drawing shows the aft face of the funnel and side aircraft hangars. The cross-hatched section is the shelter deck, which on *Bismarck* did not extend to the hull sides. *(Drawings by Miroslaw Skwiot)*

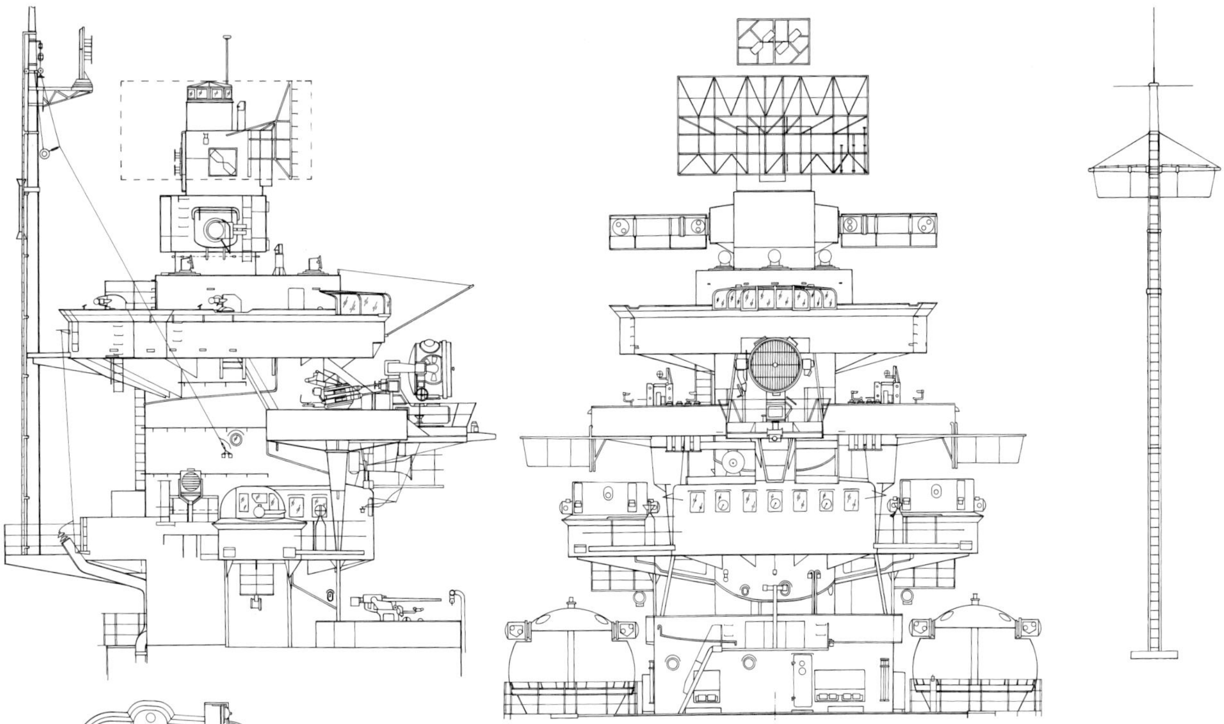

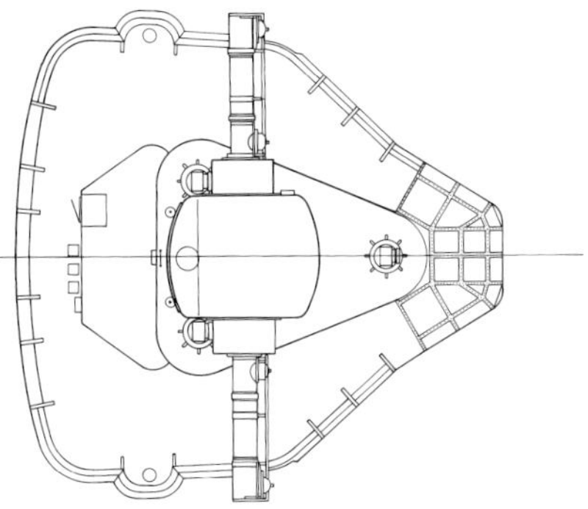

The profile, front face and plan of the forward bridge tower, along with the foremast of *Tirpitz*. These reflect the appearance after the addition in January 1942 of quad 20mm positions flanking the upper searchlight position. *(Drawings by Miroslaw Skwiot)*

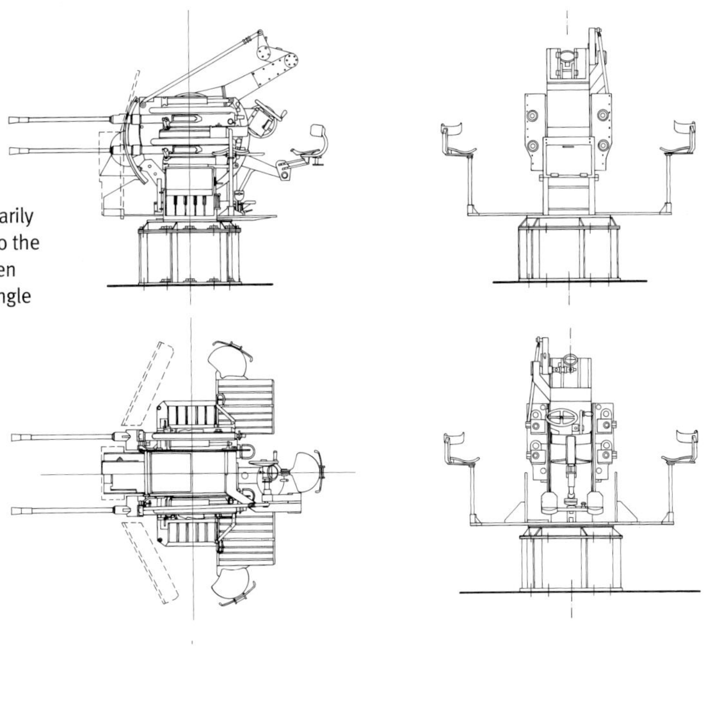

The light AA armament of the *Tirpitz* increased over time, primarily with the addition of further quadruple 20mm mounts shown to the right. By 1944 the *Tirpitz* carried eighty 20mm guns with sixteen quadruple mounts and sixteen singles. Shown below is the single 20mm carried by both ships. *(Drawings by Miroslaw Skwiot)*

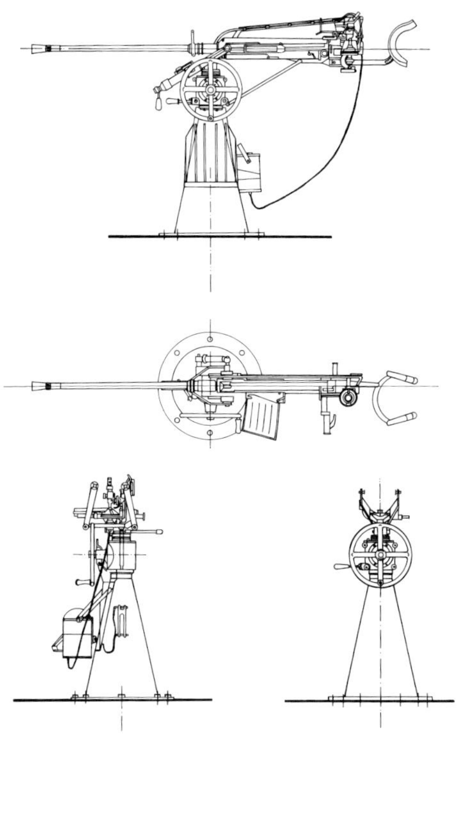

The 37mm/L83 SK C30 gun in twin mounts, for middle-range AA defence in the *Bismarck* class. *(Drawings by Miroslaw Skwiot)*

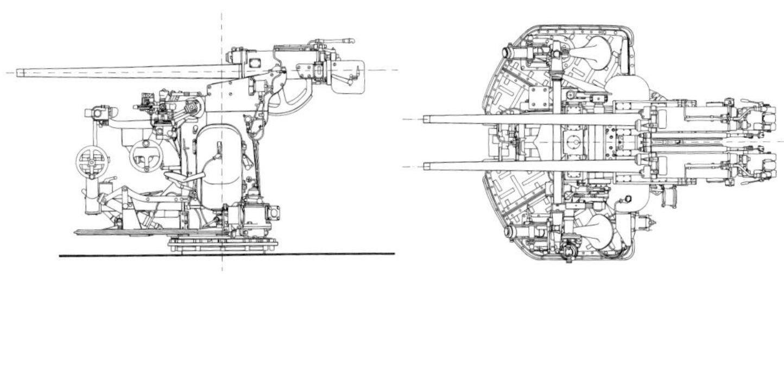

This series of drawings has profiles, plans and sections of the aft superstructure of *Tirpitz*. The cupola to the aft HA director was added in June 1941 so the open rangefinders indicate appearance before this date. One of the lower plans shows how tightly the two Arados were stored inside the main hangar.
(Drawings by Miroslaw Skwiot)

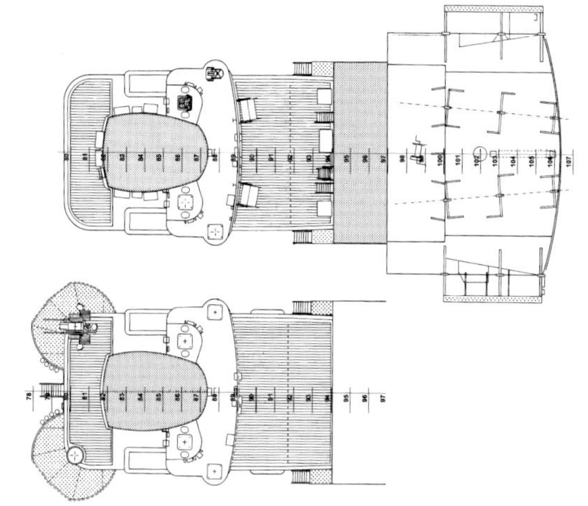

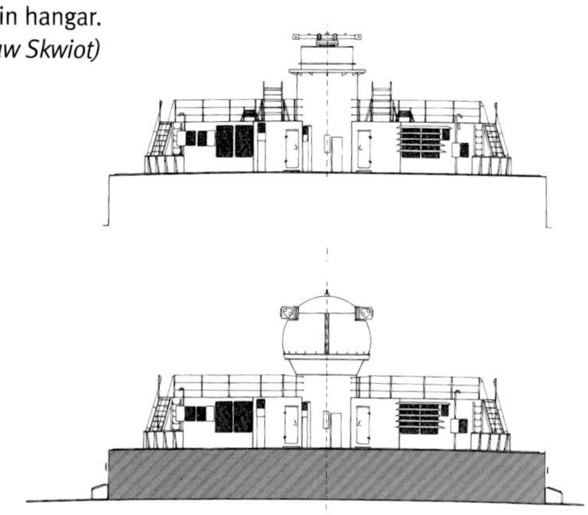

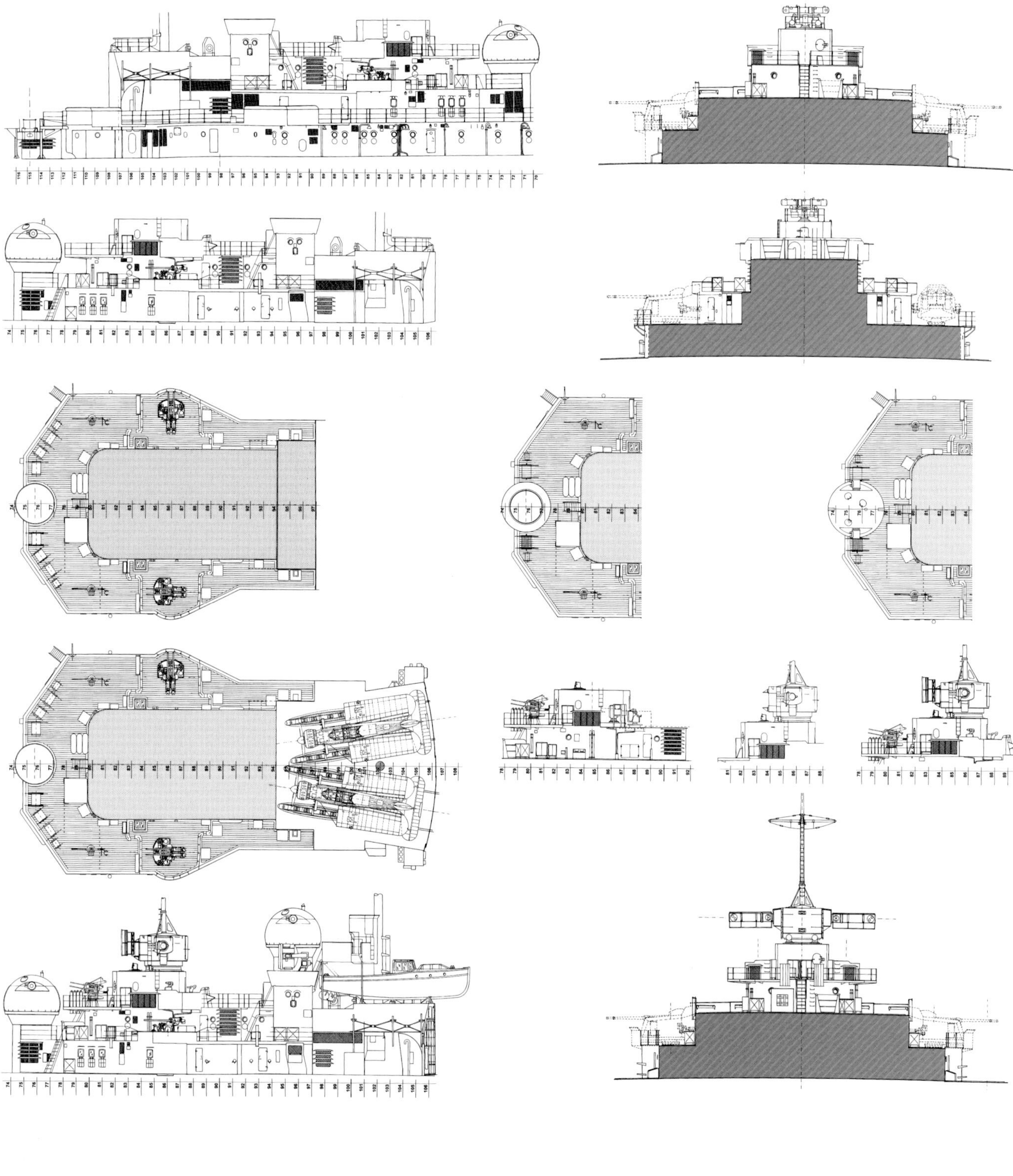

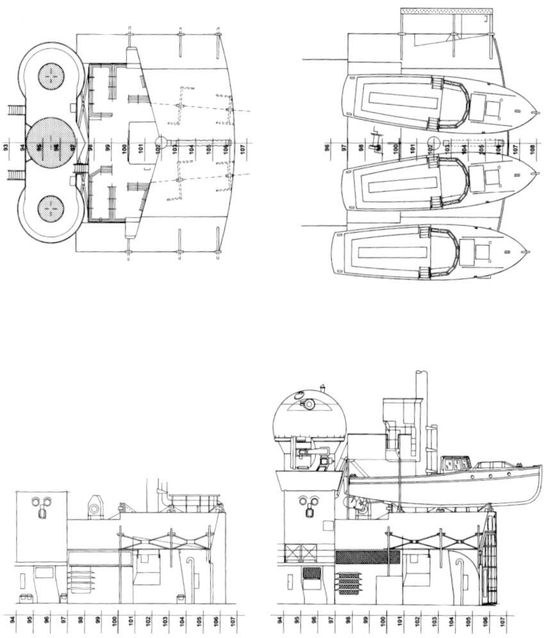

These drawings continue with the detail of fittings and positions on the aft superstructure as well as main mast of *Tirpitz*. *(Drawings by Miroslaw Skwiot)*

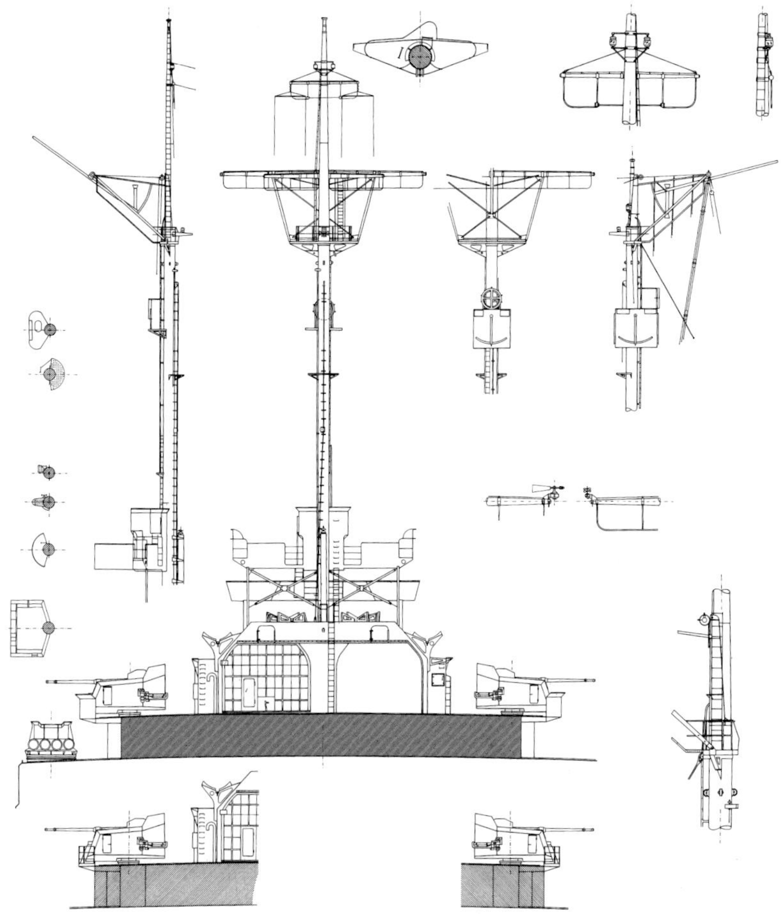

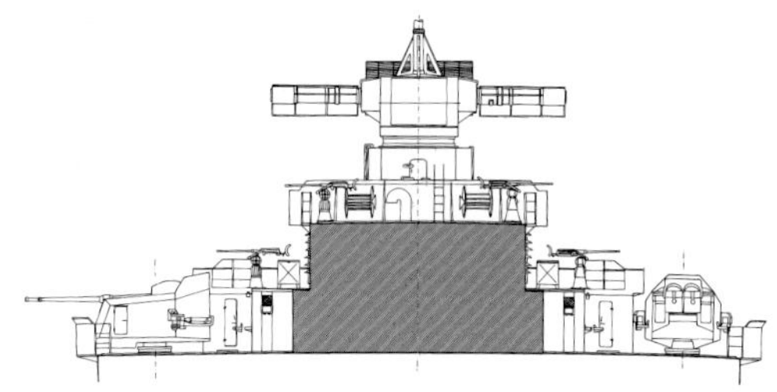

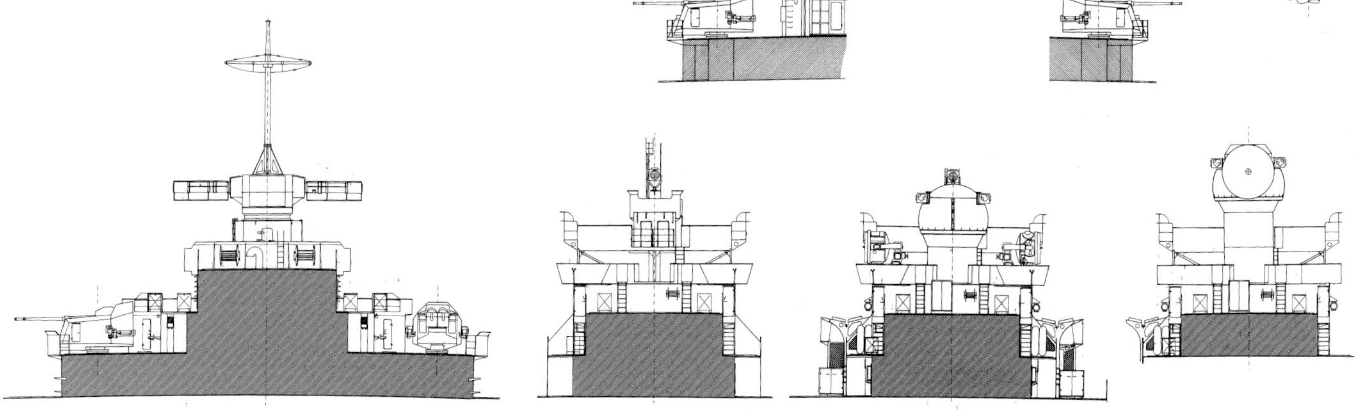

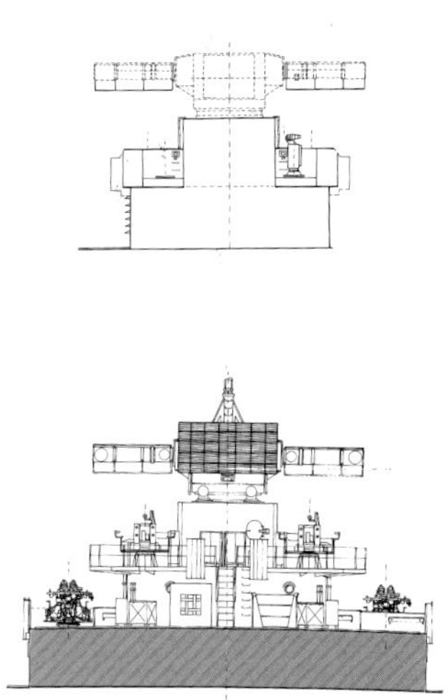

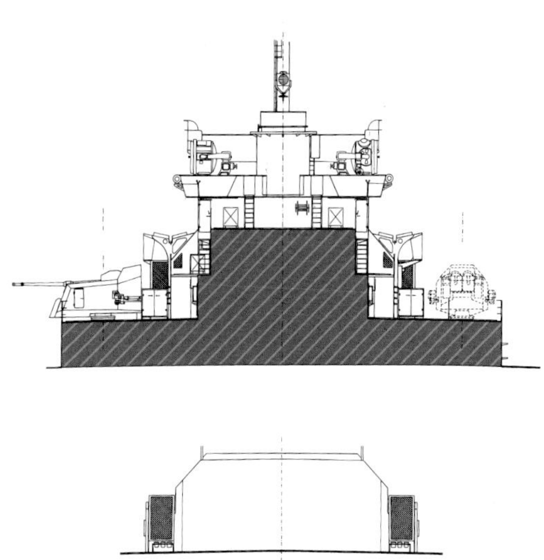

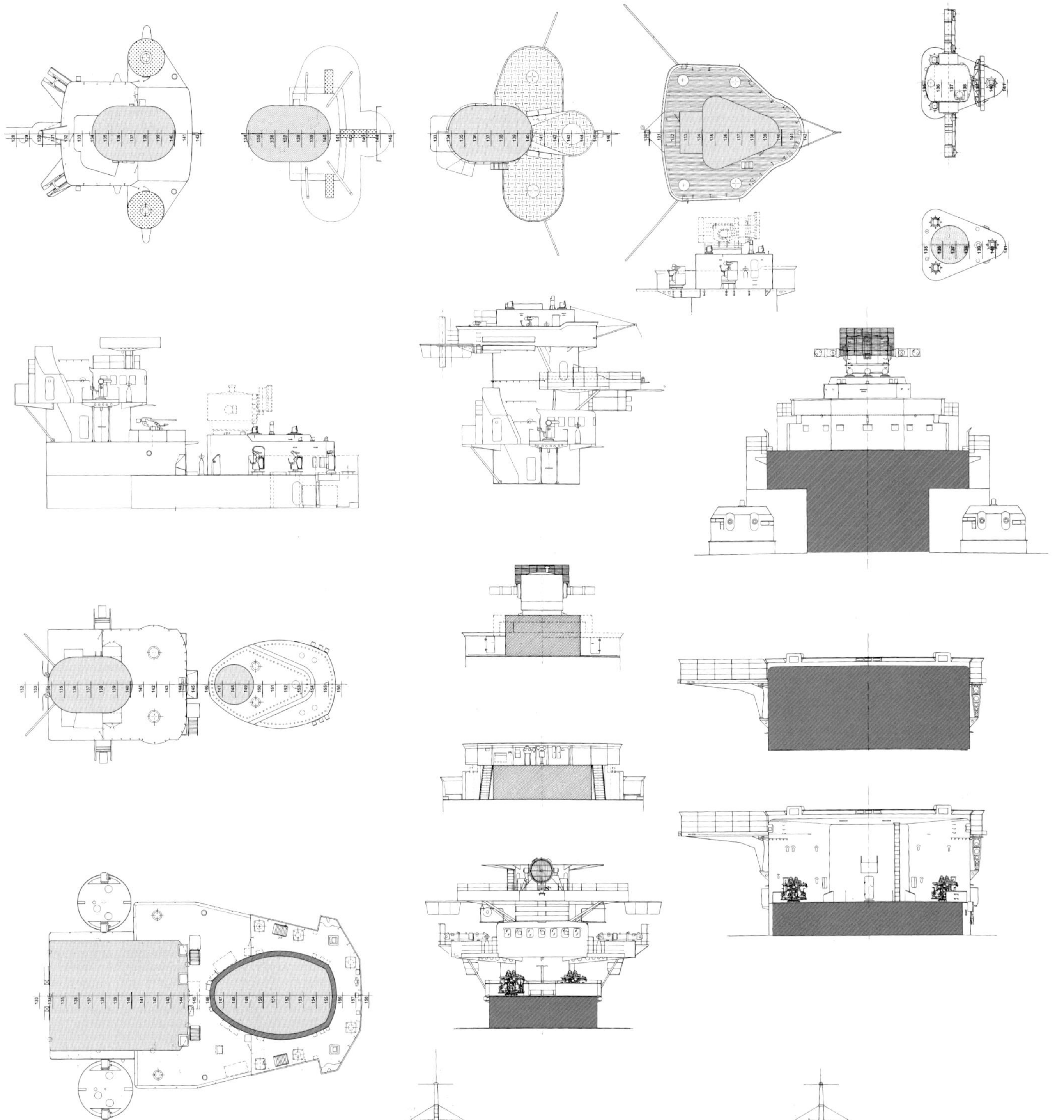

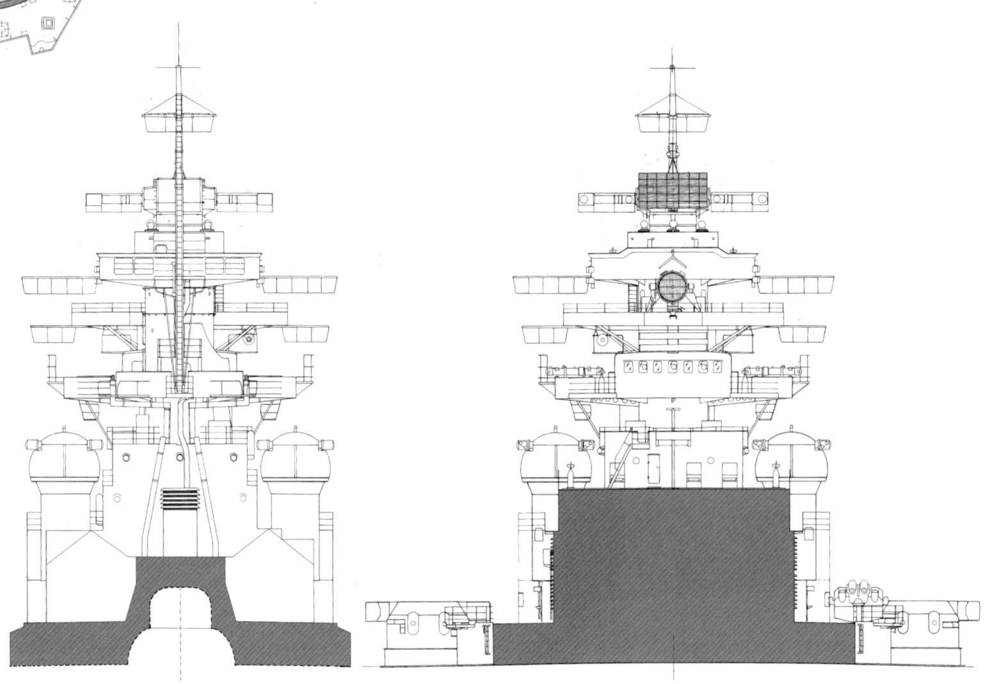

Funnel and forward tower levels, as well as frontal and aft views are shown in this series of drawings. *(Drawings by Miroslaw Skwiot)*

The Arado 196A was the standard heavy ship floatplane of the German Navy in World War Two. Five could be carried on the *Bismarck* class but only stored, with wings folded in the three hangars of the ships. With two cannons and three machine guns, this two-man floatplane was heavily armed and could carry a light bomb load. *(Drawings by Miroslaw Skwiot)*

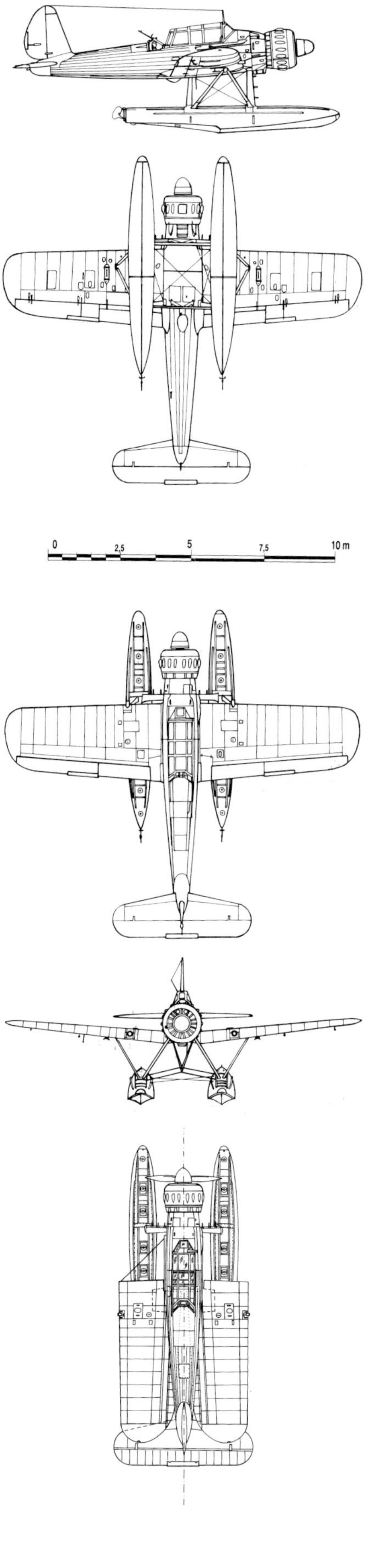

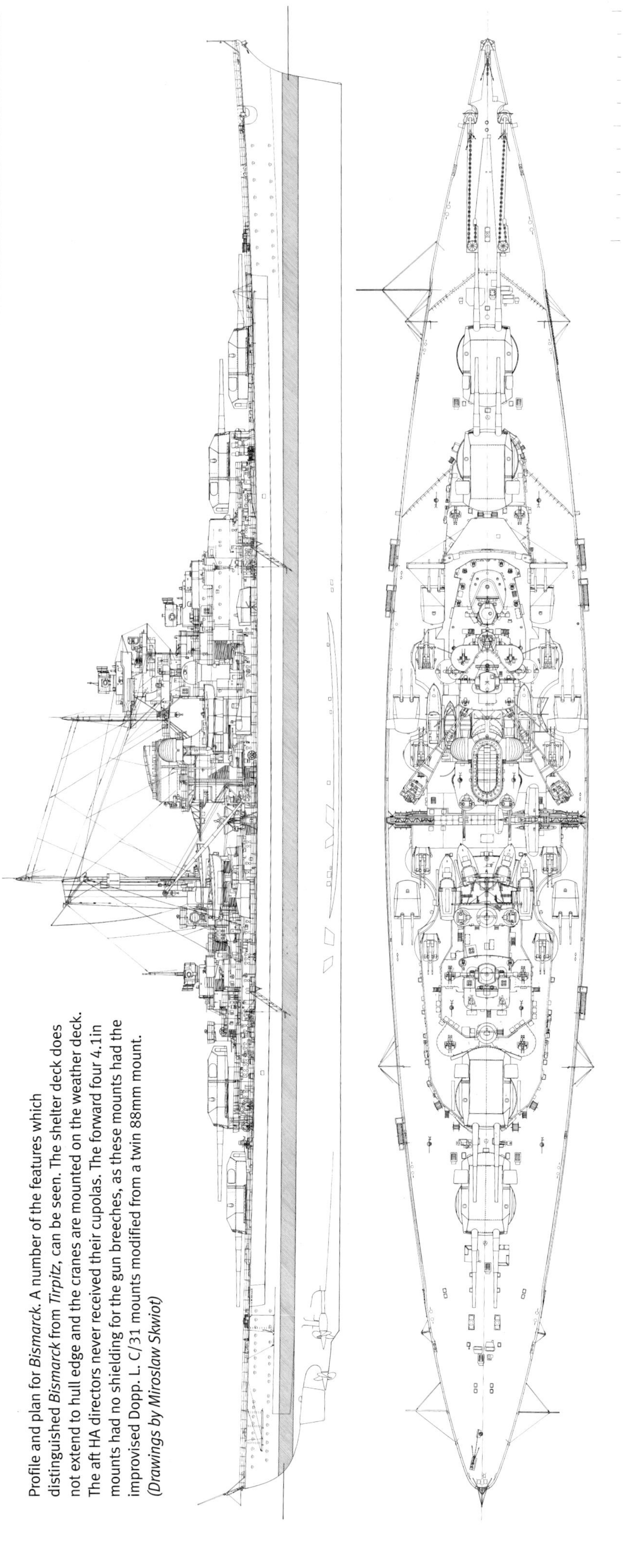

Profile and plan for *Bismarck*. A number of the features which distinguished *Bismarck* from *Tirpitz*, can be seen. The shelter deck does not extend to hull edge and the cranes are mounted on the weather deck. The aft HA directors never received their cupolas. The forward four 4.1in mounts had no shielding for the gun breeches, as these mounts had the improvised Dopp. L. C/31 mounts modified from a twin 88mm mount. *(Drawings by Miroslaw Skwiot)*

Selected References

BOOKS

Bercuson, David J and Hedwig, Holger H, *The Destruction of the Bismarck*, Overlook Trade Paperback (New York 2003)

Brennecke, Jochen, *Schlachtschiff Tirpitz, Ein Tatsachenbericht*, Heyne (Munich 1977)

Brown, David, *Tirpitz: The Floating Fortress*, Arms & Armour Press (London 1977)
A history of the ship illustrated with over 200 photos.

Brower, Jack, *Battleship Bismarck, Anatomy of the Ship*, Anova Books (London 2005)
The Anatomy of the Ship series needs no introduction: concise text, photographs and exhaustive detail drawings.

Forester, C S, *The Last Nine Days of the Bismarck*, Little, Brown and Company (Boston 1959)
The classic story woven by one of the most famed nautical writers; in the UK called *Hunting the Bismarck*.

Gallagher, Thomas, *Against All Odds: Midget Submarines Against the Tirpitz*, MacDonald (London 1971)
Story of Operation Source, in which X-Craft midget submarines successfully attacked *Tirpitz* in September 1943.

Gray, Edwyn, *Hitler's Battleships*, Naval Institute Press (Annapolis, Maryland 1999)
An easy-reading, popular history of the operational careers of the *panzerschiffe* through *Tirpitz*.

Kennedy, Ludovic, *Pursuit: The Sinking of the Bismarck*, Fontana (London 1975)
Among the best written of the histories of the *Bismarck*.

Koop, Gerhard & Scholke, Klaus-Peter, *Battleship Tirpitz*, Conway Maritime Press (London 1998)
Published in German as *Vom Originale zum modell; Schlachtschiff Tirpitz*, it provides an overview but does not go into great detail. Most of the book is comprised of photographs but there are sections on camouflage schemes with black and white profile drawings on two pages, seven pages covering a 1:100 scale model and nine pages of plans with a total of 56 pages. Fair but the AJ Press volumes by Prusinowska and Skwiot have far more intensive and informative coverage.

Mullenheim-Rechberg, Burkard, *Battleship Bismarck: A Survivor's Story*, Grafton (London 1982)
Written by the senior surviving officer of the *Bismarck*, this volume makes riveting reading – from the German perspective and by one who was there.

Preston, Antony, *The World's Worst Warships*, Conway Maritime Press (London 2002)
The author was one of the leading proponents of the proposition that the *Bismarck* was a mere rehash of the 1914 *Bayern* design. In a counter-intuitive position, he has nominated the *Bismarck* as one of the worst warship designs in the five pages on the class found in this volume.

Prusinowska, E T and Skwiot, M, *Tirpitz, Pancerniki Typu Bismarck CZ.2*, Volume 15 Encyklopedia Okretow Wojennych, AJ Press, (Gdansk, Poland 2000)
First in a five-part series on *Bismarck* and *Tirpitz*, all being superb sources for excellent photographs, plans, drawings and colour profiles and plans for both ships. Volume 15 covers the design, construction, trials and early operations of *Tirpitz* through January 1942. Text in Polish with English captions in 56 pages. Four folded sheets of superb plans in 1:400 and 1:200 scale.

Prusinowska, E T and Skwiot, M, *Tirpitz, Pancerniki Typu Bismarck CZ.2*, Volume 16 Encyklopedia Okretow Wojennych, AJ Press, (Gdansk, Poland 2001)
Volume 16 covers the operations of *Tirpitz* From March 1942 until her loss in November 1944. Text in Polish with English captions in 56 pages. Included in four separate plans are many deck and superstructure close up details.

Prusinowska, E T and Skwiot, M, *Bismarck, Pancerniki Typu Bismarck CZ.3*, Volume 17 Encyklopedia Okretow Wojennych, AJ Press, (Gdansk, Poland 2001)
Volume 17 covers the construction and operations of *Bismarck*. Text in Polish with photo captions in Polish and English in 64 pages. Included in four separate plans are profiles and plans, superstructure detail and hull lines.

Prusinowska, E T and Skwiot, M, *Bismarck/Tirpitz, Pancerniki Typu Bismarck CZ.4*, Volume 18 Encyklopedia Okretow Wojennych, AJ Press, (Gdansk, Poland 2002)
Volume 18 covers additional information on *Bismarck* and *Tirpitz* with emphasis on fittings through excellent photographs. Text in Polish with photo captions in Polish and English in 64 pages. Numerous details of *Bismarck* and *Tirpitz* on four separate folded plans.

Prusinowska, E T and Skwiot, M, *Bismarck/Tirpitz, Pancerniki Typu Bismarck CZ.5*, Volume 19 Encyklopedia Okretow Wojennych, AJ Press, (Gdansk, Poland 2003)
Volume 19 covers armament and fittings with outstanding onboard photographs and detailed CAD drawings of armament. Text in Polish with photo captions in Polish and English in 84 pages. Four sheets of detailed plans, plus two sheets of glorious colour CAD graphics of *Bismarck's* superstructure.

Schmalenbach, Paul, *Warships in Profile Volume 2, Kriegsmarine Bismarck*, Profile Publications (Windsor UK, 1973)
First published separately in softbound format and then incorporated in the hardbound yearly compilation of the *Warships in Profile* titles. The monograph is 28 pages in length and provides a good mixture of text and photographs. A nice four-page colour profile and plan is the centerfold of the volume but it misses certain small details such as bow outboard anchor fairings and depicts all 105mm mounts on C37 mounts.

Wiper, Steve, *Kriegsmarine Bismarck, Warship Pictorial 19*, Classic Warships Publishing (Tucson, Arizona 2003)
There are 72 pages of excellent, informative photographs with extensively annotated captions. Photographs, including colour photographs of the ship in September 1940, show overall portraits of the ship as well as many detailed shots of armament, fittings and equipment. It provides ideal coverage for the modeller. Also included are beautiful CAD drawings by Thomas Schmid.

Wiper, Steve, *Kriegsmarine Tirpitz, Warship Pictorial 26*, Classic Warships Publishing (Tucson, Arizona 2006)
The same format is used as found in the previous release on *Bismarck*. There are 72 pages of excellent, informative photographs with extensively annotated captions. Photographs show overall portraits of the ship as well as many detailed shots of armament, fittings and equipment.

WEBSITES OF CONTRIBUTORS

www.alnavco.com
www.collnav.de
www.dragonmodelsusa.com
www.freetimehobbies.com
www.larsenal.com/
www.lionroar.net
www.pacificfront.com
www.voyagermodel.com
www.whiteensignmodels.com

OTHER WEBSITES OF INTEREST

www.bismarck-class.dk/index.html
www.bobhenneman.info/Tirpitzwreck.htm
www.feldgrau.com/kriegs.html
www.german-navy.de/kriegsmarine/index.html
www.kbismarck.com/
www.kriegsmarine-reich.co.uk/
www.lancastermuseum.ca/tirpitz.html
www.raf.mod.uk/bombercommand/tirpitz.html